THE POWER OF PASSIVE INCOME

How to Build Wealth with Minimal Effort

O.G. CEO

Photo Credit: iStock Free Images

Cover design by: Art Painter

Link to "The Millionaire Mindset" by O.G. CEO

https://www.amazon.com/dp/B0BZSMSVN5

Dedication

This great and wealth-transforming book is dedicated to everyone who will employ the principles in this book to maximize the power of passive income and navigate the path of building wealth with minimal effort.

Table of Content

Dedication

Introduction

Reasons Why This Book Is Important

Who This Book Is For

Chapter 1

The Basics of Passive Income

Recognizing the Nature of Passive Income

Active vs Passive Income: Pros and Cons

Misconceptions & Fallacies Concerning Passive Income

Chapter 2

Diverse Sources of Passive Income

Real Estate Investment Income

Earnings from the Bank and Certificate of Deposits as Interest

Income from the exploitation of intellectual property

Affiliate Marketing Revenue

Peer-to-Peer Lending Income

Chapter 3

Creating a Portfolio for Passive Income

Setting Objectives for Passive Income

Finding Your Comfort Level With Risk

Choose Which Sources of Passive Income Will Best Suit Your Needs

Incorporating Diversification Into Your Investment Strategy

Building Several Sources of Passive Income

Chapter 4

Income from Real Estate Investment

How to Pick a Good Investment Property

Funding Your Property Purchase

Methods for Selecting an Appropriate Property

How to Take Care of Your Rental Home

Optimizing Your Rental Profits

Chapter 5

Earning Passive Income from Stocks and Bonds

Stocks and Bonds: Everything You Need to Know

Investing Wisely in Stocks and Bonds

Investment Portfolio Construction

Taking Charge of Your Financial Investments

Paying Dividends Back into the Market

Chapter 6

Generating Passive Income from IP

Legal Aspects of Intellectual Property

Putting Pen to Paper (or Screen) for Books, Digital Editions, and Audiobooks

Making and Marketing Digital Courses

Software Development and Distribution

Everything You Need to Know About Selling Your Recordings, Paintings, and Photos Under a License

Chapter 7

Affiliate Marketing as a Source of Passive Income

The Basics of Affiliate Marketing

A Guide to Choose the Best Affiliate Programs

Producing High-Quality Material for Advertising Purposes

Building and Expanding Your Fanbase

Keeping Tabs on the Outcomes of Your Affiliate Marketing Efforts

Chapter 8

Earning Money While You Sleep: Peer-to-Peer Lending

Learning About P2P Loans

Methods for Deciding on a Reliable Online Lending Service

Criteria for Judging Loans and Borrowers

Taking Charge of Your Loan Portfolio

Profitability while limiting exposure to lose.

Chapter 9

Optimizing Your Sources of Passive Income

Multiplying Your Sources of Passive Income

Generating Passive Income Via Automation

Financial Planning for Passive Income

Using Passive Income to Fund Retirement

Using Passive Income to Create Generational Wealth

Chapter 10

  Last Thoughts

    Important Takeaways

    Motivating Ideas and Words of Advice for Getting Things Done

    Methods and Materials for Generating Passive Income

Conclusions and Future Directions

Introduction

Achieving financial independence through passive income streams is the subject of **The Power of Passive Income: How to Build Wealth with Minimal Effort**, an instructional handbook. This book aims to help readers learn about the various forms of passive income, how to construct a diversified portfolio, and how to maximize their returns with the least work. If you follow the advice in this book, you may set yourself up with a steady stream of passive income that will last for years to come.

Reasons Why This Book Is Important

In today's economy, it's customary to achieve financial stability by relying on traditional types of income. For many people, the necessity of diversifying their sources of income has arisen in response to the rising cost of living and the growing instability of their employment prospects. Passive income streams are a practical and effective strategy to combat this issue and help people accomplish their financial independence goals. This book aims to provide readers with the information they need to set up and maintain passive income sources.

Who This Book Is For

Anybody interested in gaining independence from their financial situation through the development of passive income sources. It's great for people who want to earn extra money on the side, establish a secure means of financial support for themselves, or amass riches over time. No matter how much or how little experience you have with investing, the information in this book will be useful. This book will help you understand passive income and use it to accumulate wealth with little effort.

Suppose you want to take charge of your financial future. In that case, you need to read The Power of Passive Income: How to Build Wealth with Minimal Effort. Achieving financial freedom is within reach of any reader of this book because of the practical guidance, compelling examples, and tried-and-true methods presented in this book. You can learn more about passive income and how to create a varied portfolio that fits your needs and goals if you take the time to investigate the various forms it can take.

This book's straightforward approach makes it suitable for readers with varying degrees of expertise in the financial realm. This book simplifies difficult financial topics and provides actionable advice that may be put to use immediately. This book is ideal for those who wish to earn wealth without effort, such as busy professionals, entrepreneurs, or anyone who wants to generate a passive income stream.

To sum up, The Power of Passive Income: How to Build Wealth with Minimal Effort is a must-read for everyone interested in gaining financial independence through passive income sources. This book equips you with the information and abilities to develop a sustainable and consistent stream of income that can help you reach your financial objectives through its thorough coverage of the issue, concrete recommendations, and examples.

CHAPTER 1

The Basics of Passive Income

1. Recognizing the Nature of Passive Income

2. Active vs Passive Income: Pros and Cons

3. Misconceptions and Fallacies Concerning Passive Income

The concept of "passive income" has gained prominence in recent years, especially among individuals aiming for greater economic autonomy. Although the concept of passive income is familiar, many people's understanding of what it is and how it is earned remains hazy at best.

Passive income is money received in exchange for doing very little work, such as rent, dividends, interest, or royalties. It's become clear that in today's economy, the majority of people can't get by on their primary source of income alone. Hence the concept of passive income has gained prominence.

This chapter will introduce passive income and discuss its benefits and drawbacks. Several misconceptions and fallacies concerning passive income will also be dispelled.

Recognizing the Nature of Passive Income

Earning money with little to no effort is called passive income. It's distinct from the money you bring in by actively working at a job or running a business. Mailbox money describes the passive revenue that can be made even when one is sleeping or on vacation.

Rental income from real estate, dividends from stocks and bonds, interest from savings and CDs, royalties from intellectual property, affiliate marketing income, and peer-to-peer lending income are all examples of passive income.

Earning passive income is defined by the fact that it calls for minimal effort on your part. This indicates that the person will continue to earn money with little to no additional effort once the first work has been done to establish the income stream. To give just one example, once a rental property has been purchased and rented out, the landlord will get monthly rental money without having to do anything.

Passive Income and Its Varieties

Many forms of passive income have different pros and cons.

The following are examples of popular passive income sources:

Earnings from renting out a home or apartment are examples of rental revenue. Rental terms for the property are flexible and can be either short or long-term. Since it can be counted every month, rental income is a common source of passive income.

Investments in stocks and bonds that pay dividends produce dividend income. A dividend is a distribution of a company's earnings to its stockholders. As long as the investor purchases high-quality stocks and bonds that pay dividends consistently, dividend income can be a stable source of passive income.

Investing in savings accounts, certificates of deposit, and other interest-bearing investments can generate interest income. Despite the current low-interest rate environment, interest income can still be a stable passive income source, especially for people who value security and predictability above rapid growth and huge returns.

Earnings from licensing works of intellectual property, such as books, songs, and computer programs, are known as royalties. If one has developed in-demand intellectual property and is entitled to royalties, then one can expect a reliable source of passive income.

Profits from affiliate marketing: In affiliate marketing, one promotes the goods or services of another business in exchange for a cut of the sales generated. Affiliate marketing could be a great way to earn money on autopilot if you have a large audience.

Earnings from P2P Lending: This kind of financing comprises the borrowing and lending of money between private individuals or small enterprises via the Internet. Loan interest is a form of passive income for investors.

In conclusion, passive income is money produced with minimal effort on your part. Rental income, dividend income, interest income, royalties, affiliate marketing income, and P2P lending income are examples of this type of money coming in. Individuals can tailor their passive income streams to their circumstances and objectives by familiarizing themselves with the various options available. One way to achieve financial independence and freedom is to construct a portfolio of passive income streams that generates money on autopilot.

Active vs Passive Income: Pros and Cons

As more and more people strive for financial autonomy and the freedom to earn money without exerting much effort, the concept of passive income has gained widespread attention in recent years. Though passive income has numerous benefits, there are also some drawbacks. This chapter will discuss the pros and cons of passive income.

Profits from Passive Activities

The independence and adaptability that come with a passive income stream are two of its primary benefits. Passive income allows people to make money without actively working for it, freeing them up to focus on other aspects of their lives.

Because those earning passive income aren't linked to a single, time-consuming endeavor, they're less likely to experience burnout and stress as a result of their work. This has the potential to boost health all around.

Individuals can become less reliant on any one source of income by establishing many passive income streams.

Having a steady stream of passive income to rely on for day-to-day living needs or as a cushion in the event of an emergency or job loss is one way to feel more secure about one's financial future.

Get as much as you want with passive income if you're ready to put in the work to establish the system in the first place.

Problems with Passive Income

Although passive income has the potential to be a reliable source of income over the long term, it usually requires an initial commitment to getting things rolling. For people without ready access to capital, this may be an insurmountable hurdle.

Passive income sources, such as investments in stocks or real estate, can carry their share of risk and uncertainty. The possibility of loss is constantly present, and it's tough for risk-averse people to deal with.

Although the individual is often dependent on external factors like market conditions or client demand, passive income streams might also lack a certain level of control. Some people would want to have more direct influence over their income and find this situation annoying.

Putting together a reliable source of passive income can take some time and work at the outset. Those who don't have the time or money to put into the initial setup may find this to be an obstacle.

Although passive income streams can be a reliable funding source, there may be restrictions on how much money can be made from them. For instance, the amount of money that can be made through renting out a property or collecting dividends is restricted by the number of shares that are owned.

In conclusion, passive income has many benefits, including portability, independence, lower levels of stress and burnout, higher levels of financial stability, more prospective earnings, and the ability to work less. There are, however, drawbacks to think about, such as the need for up-front investment, risks, and uncertainties, a loss of control, a protracted setup process, and a modest revenue ceiling. Individuals can decide if passive income is the best option for them and how to establish a profitable and diversified portfolio of passive income streams by weighing the pros and cons.

Misconceptions & Fallacies Concerning Passive Income

The term "passive income" has gained popularity in recent years as more people look for ways to become financially independent and get resources without actively seeking them out. Many people have false assumptions regarding passive income because of common myths and misunderstandings. We'll dispel some of the most widespread misconceptions about passive income in this section.

First Fallacy: Passive Income Is Simple Gain

There is a widespread misconception that passive income can be generated quickly and easily with minimal effort. While it's true that passive income streams can pay well in the long run, they often necessitate a large time commitment and financial outlay to initiate. To start a profitable rental property business, for instance, you'll need to look for and buy properties, manage tenants, and do necessary repairs and maintenance. Producing high-quality content, growing an audience, and advertising the blog or podcast through multiple means are all necessary steps in making either a blog or podcast successful. Although passive income can be reliable over time, there are other means to amass wealth.

Second fallacy: Passive income does not require any active effort.

The idea that passive income can be earned with little effort or upkeep is another frequent misconception. While some forms of passive income may require less regular upkeep than others, all sources of income will need to be managed and maintained at some point. Maintaining rental properties and addressing tenant issues is a continuous process, just as keeping an eye on the stock market and the performance of companies that provide dividends is. Though passive income can indeed give you more leeway than a 9-to-5 job, it still needs to be more hands-off.

False Belief #3: Only the wealthy may benefit from passive income

One more fallacy about passive income is that it's out of reach for everyone but the well-off. While some forms of passive income, like real estate investing, may necessitate a sizable initial outlay of capital, many other forms of passive income can be initiated with very little, or no, an outlay of capital at all. A computer and an internet connection are all that is needed to start a successful blog or podcast, and a website or social media account is all that is needed to start making money through affiliate marketing. With the right strategy and approach, anyone can begin building passive income, and while financial resources can make it easier to build a diversified portfolio of passive income streams, anyone can do it.

The fourth most common myth is that only certain types of individuals can make a living from passive income.

There is also the false belief that only business owners and investors can benefit from passive income. In truth, people from all walks of life and levels of expertise may establish passive income streams. The term "passive income" refers to earnings from investments that need little to no active management on the part of the investor. There is no one-size-fits-all approach to creating passive income, and anyone can find a strategy that works for them. However, certain skills or knowledge may help create certain types of passive income streams.

Fifth Fallacy: Passive Income Is Consistently Earning

Finally, one of the most widespread misunderstandings about passive income is the belief that it is always stable and can be relied upon. While passive income streams have the potential to be stable, long-term income generators, they are nonetheless vulnerable to market fluctuations and other risks associated with investing. Dividend income, for instance, may be affected by market circumstances or the performance of the company that pays it, and vacancies in rental properties may occur. Having a varied income portfolio can help minimize risk and boost stability. Therefore, it's vital to carefully consider the risks and potential returns of any passive income stream before investing time or money in it.

In conclusion, there are numerous myths and misconceptions regarding the passive income that might lead to high expectations or misunderstandings about what it takes to construct successful passive income streams. In light of the truths of passive income, such as the

CHAPTER 2

Diverse Sources of Passive Income

1. Income from Real Estate Rentals Interest and Dividends from Investments

2. Earnings from the Bank and Certificate of Deposits as Interest

3. Income from the exploitation of intellectual property

4. Earnings from Online Advertising Revenue from P2P Lending

Real Estate Investment Income

One of the most common and widely recognized types of passive income is rental revenue from real estate. Rental income from real estate can be reliable and stable, and there's always the chance that the value of the investment can rise over time. In this chapter, we will discuss how to start a profitable rental property business, as well as the advantages and disadvantages of real estate rental revenue.

Gains from Real Estate Rental Revenue

The possibility for passive income over the long term is a major perk of real estate rental revenue. Monthly rental income from an investment property can be used to pay the mortgage, improve the building, or put away for other ventures. In addition to the stability and income that rental properties give, they also offer the chance for long-term capital appreciation as property values rise.

Possible tax benefits are another perk of renting income from real estate. Mortgage interest, property taxes, insurance, and maintenance and repairs are all tax-deductible expenses for landlords, allowing them to save money and boost their rental property's profitability.

Earning a living through rental property presents some difficult situations.

Rental property revenue has the potential to bring in extra cash, but it also has its own set of difficulties. Finding and keeping tenants is a major headache for landlords. Landlords face several responsibilities, including the time-consuming and difficult process of tenant screening and the management of ongoing maintenance and repairs, as well as tenant concerns.

As an added downside, some investors may be put off by the high initial cost of buying rental property. Mortgage payments, taxes, insurance, and maintenance costs are only some of the recurring costs associated with owning real estate. Investors need to be sure that the rental revenue is sufficient to cover these costs and create a positive cash flow before purchasing a rental property.

Tips for Establishing a Successful Real Estate Rental Agency

There are various ways to increase your rental revenue from real estate, despite the many obstacles you may face. Preliminary due diligence on prospective real estate purchases is crucial. Before buying, investors should think about the property's location, rental revenue possibilities, operating costs, and the state of the market. If you need help determining whether or not a property is a viable investment, consulting with a real estate agent or management firm can be useful.

Property and tenant management is another crucial tactic. As part of this process, you will be responsible for tenant screening, regular property maintenance, and responding quickly to tenant complaints. Working with a property management business can be beneficial for many landlords since it allows them to delegate day-to-day tasks related to the property and renters.

Last but not least, you must have a plan for the future of your rental property business. To do this, one can either keep the rental revenue and reinvest it into the property to increase its value, add more rental properties to the portfolio, or sell the property at a profit. Having a plan in place can aid in making sound investment choices and guaranteeing the rental property business's long-term profitability.

Last but not least, for those willing to put in the work, rental income from real estate can be a lucrative source of passive income for investors. Real estate investment is a popular option for those who want to develop wealth with little time or effort because of the long-term income and capital gain it may provide. Investors can attain financial independence through passive income from real estate by building a successful rental property business through rigorous evaluation of potential properties, good management of the property and renters, and a long-term strategy.

Capital Gains and Interest Payments on Bonds and Stocks

Stock and bond dividends are other common sources of passive income for investors. When a company or government agency pays out a percentage of its earnings to its stockholders or bondholders, it is known as a dividend. In this chapter, we'll discuss how to construct a dividend income portfolio, as well as the advantages and disadvantages of dividend income from stocks and bonds.

Gains from Stock and Bond Dividends

Dividends from stocks and bonds can be an excellent source of passive income because of this. Dividends from corporations and governments can be collected on a quarterly or annual basis and used to pay bills, add to an investment portfolio, or put away for the future. Although dividend payments have the potential to grow over time and mitigate the effects of inflation, stocks and bonds that pay dividends can be a useful hedging tool.

Dividend income from stocks and bonds also offers the chance for financial appreciation. Investments that pay dividends are one way to earn passive income, but stocks and bonds also have the potential to grow in value. If the stock or bond is sold at a profit, the investor receives additional funds.

Diverse Stocks and Bonds Provide Difficult Dividend Income Opportunities

Dividends from stocks and bonds can help in many ways, but they also present their unique issues. Dividend income faces significant hurdles, chief among them the inherent dangers of investing in stocks and bonds. Both stock and bond prices are vulnerable to market forces, and in times of financial stress for companies or governments, dividends may be lowered or even canceled.

Having to pay taxes on dividends is another potential complication. Investment returns may be dampened since dividends are taxed at a higher rate than ordinary income. Investors need to know how much tax they will owe on dividends and how to budget for it.

Tips for Building a Robust Dividend Portfolio

There are various ways to construct a profitable dividend income portfolio despite the difficulties of dividends from equities and bonds. High-quality dividend-paying stocks and bonds are a must and should be one of your primary investments. Companies and governments with a history of consistent dividend payments, solid financial footing, and promising future growth should be prioritized by investors.

Diversifying sources of dividend income is another crucial tactic. Spreading your money out among multiple equities and bonds in various markets can help you diversify your risk and boost your long-term income and capital gain potential.

Finally, a dividend income portfolio needs a long-term plan. Investment returns can be maximized in several ways, including reinvesting dividends to expand the portfolio or selling appreciated holdings to fund new investments. To guarantee the long-term success of a dividend income portfolio, it is important to have a clear plan to guide investment selections.

In sum, investors who put in the time and effort to develop a good dividend income portfolio can benefit from dividend income from stocks and bonds. Investing in stocks and bonds is a popular option for those who want to develop wealth with little work due to the potential for long-term income and capital appreciation. An investor can achieve financial independence through dividend income from stocks and bonds by picking high-quality dividend-paying equities and bonds, diversifying the portfolio, and having a long-term strategy in place.

Earnings from the Bank and Certificate of Deposits as Interest

Investors can also earn passive income through interest income from savings accounts and CDs. Interest is a percentage of the principal balance paid by a bank or credit union on a savings or certificate of deposit. This chapter will discuss the merits and pitfalls of interest income from savings accounts and CDs, as well as methods for maximizing returns.

Cashing in on the Rewards of Interest from Savings and Certificates of Deposit

Interest earnings from safe investments like savings accounts and certificates of deposit (CDs) have several advantages. Savings accounts and CDs give a guaranteed return on investment, in contrast to stocks and bonds, whose value might change depending on market conditions. Therefore, they are favored by those looking for a passive income stream with minimal risk.

Earning interest from savings and CDs is great, and there's also the bonus of being able to withdraw the money whenever you choose. There is a vast variety of savings and certificate of deposit accounts available at many different banks and financial institutions. Investors can select the savings account or CD that is most suitable for their situation and long-term objectives.

Problems Associated with Interest Earned on Savings and Certificates of Deposit

Having a steady stream of interest from CDs and savings accounts can be helpful in several ways, but it also has its unique issues. The relatively low rate of return on interest income, in comparison to other investment options, is one of its major drawbacks. Guaranteed returns from savings accounts and CDs are lower than those from riskier investments like equities and bonds.

The value of an investment made using interest income may be threatened by inflation. Even if the interest rate is fixed for the duration of the loan, it may still fall short of keeping up with inflation. This indicates that the investment's purchasing power may decline over time, cutting into the investment's potential return on investment.

Methods for Getting the Most Out of Your Interest Income from Savings and Certificates of Deposit

Notwithstanding the difficulties of earning interest on savings and certificates of deposit, there are numerous methods for increasing profits. Examining competing interest rate offers is a crucial step. It's vital to shop around for the best interest rate possible on savings accounts and certificates of deposit (CDs) because rates vary widely between banks and other financial organizations.

Consider the CD's expiration date as a different tactic. Certificates of deposit (CDs) are investments that require the holder to lock away their money for a specified period in exchange for a higher interest rate than what is available with a savings account. Investors can potentially receive a better rate of return by purchasing a longer-term CD, but they will have less access to their funds.

Furthermore, analyzing the fees connected with savings accounts and CDs is vital. Several banks and financial organizations charge fees for holding a savings account or CD, which can lower the total profitability of the investment. Investors should carefully check the terms and conditions of their savings account or CD to ensure that they are not being charged excessive fees.

In conclusion, interest income from savings accounts and CDs can be a significant passive income source for investors seeking a low-risk investment alternative. While problems and hazards are involved with investing in savings accounts and CDs, the flexibility and low risk connected with these investments make them a popular alternative for investors trying to create wealth with minimal effort. By shopping around for the best interest rates, choosing the correct duration for the CD, and carefully evaluating costs, investors can maximize their returns and attain financial independence through passive income from savings accounts and CDs.

Income from the exploitation of intellectual property

Royalties from intellectual property are another source of passive income that artists and innovators can obtain. Intellectual property comprises copyrights, patents, trademarks, and trade secrets, and can be licensed or sold to others in exchange for royalties. In this chapter, we will cover the benefits and problems of receiving royalties from intellectual property, as well as some tactics for maximizing profits.

Advantages of Royalties from Intellectual Property

One of the major benefits of generating royalties from intellectual property is the possibility of substantial profits. Creators and innovators who control the rights to important intellectual property can earn considerable royalties by licensing or selling those rights to others. This can provide a consistent source of passive income over the long term as long as the intellectual property stays valued.

Another benefit of earning royalties from intellectual property is the flexibility of these investments. Creators and innovators can opt to license or sell their intellectual property to others, allowing them to generate cash without actively managing or operating a firm. This might be especially advantageous for persons who need more time or resources to start and maintain a business.

Difficulties of Royalties from Intellectual Property

While royalties from an intellectual property can provide many benefits, there are also certain challenges involved with this sort of passive income. One of the main issues is the high expense of obtaining and preserving intellectual property. Creators and innovators may need to invest large amounts of time and money in establishing their intellectual property, as well as securing patents or trademarks to safeguard their rights.

Another area for improvement in obtaining royalties from intellectual property is the potential for infringement. Intellectual property can be difficult to protect, and artists and inventors may need to take legal action to prevent others from utilizing or replicating their intellectual property without permission. This can be a time-consuming and expensive process and affect the investment's profitability.

Techniques for Maximizing Earnings on Royalties from Intellectual Property

Even with the difficulty of obtaining royalties from intellectual property, several techniques exist for maximizing revenues. One of the most important methods is to properly evaluate the potential worth of intellectual property before investing considerable time and money into its development. Creators and inventors should perform market research and estimate the future demand for their intellectual property to ensure that it is worth the expenditure.

Another key technique is to safeguard intellectual property through patents, trademarks, or copyrights. This can assist prevent others from exploiting or copying the intellectual property without permission and can help ensure that the creator or inventor obtains a fair share of the income created by the intellectual property.

Finally, choosing a suitable licensing or selling approach for intellectual property is crucial. Creators and innovators can opt to license their intellectual property to others, allowing them to generate cash without giving up ownership of the property. Alternatively, they can choose to sell the intellectual property altogether, which can generate a single sum payment but may not provide ongoing passive income.

In conclusion, royalties from an intellectual property can be a beneficial source of passive income for creators and innovators who control the rights to valuable intellectual property. While there are hurdles and hazards connected with collecting royalties from intellectual property, the potential for high returns and the flexibility of these investments make them a popular alternative for individuals trying to grow wealth with minimal work. By carefully evaluating the potential value of the intellectual property, protecting it through patents or trademarks, and choosing the right licensing or selling strategy, creators and inventors can maximize their returns and achieve financial independence through passive income from intellectual property.

Affiliate Marketing Revenue

Affiliate marketing is another common strategy for creating passive income, and it involves promoting items or services on behalf of other businesses in exchange for a commission. In this chapter, we will cover the pros and challenges of earning income through affiliate marketing, as well as some tactics for maximizing returns.

Advantages of Affiliate Marketing Income

One of the main benefits of affiliate marketing is the freedom it affords. Affiliates can choose to advertise items or services in a wide range of industries and can do so from anywhere with an internet connection. This makes it a perfect passive income source for folks who love working from home or on their schedule.

Another perk of affiliate marketing is the possibility of significant profits. Affiliates can earn commissions of up to 50% or more for each sale they produce, depending on the product or service being marketed. This can provide a steady source of passive income over the long term as long as the items or services being pushed remain popular and in demand.

Difficulties of Affiliate Marketing Income

While affiliate marketing can give numerous benefits, some challenges are also involved with this sort of passive income. One of the main obstacles is competition. Affiliates must compete with other affiliates to advertise the same products or services. They may need to invest substantial time and money into cultivating an audience and establishing their name in their chosen field.

Another problem with affiliate marketing is the potential for fraud. Certain merchants may engage in fraudulent acts, such as changing the conditions of their affiliate programs or failing to pay commissions on time or in whole. Affiliates must thoroughly investigate the merchants they choose to partner with to verify that they are legitimate and trustworthy.

Ways for Maximizing Returns on Affiliate Marketing Money

Despite the hurdles of earning cash with affiliate marketing, there are several ways to maximize returns. One of the most crucial methods is to identify the correct items or services to promote. Affiliates should investigate the demand for products or services in their chosen business, as well as the commission rates and terms of the affiliate programs offered by various merchants.

Another powerful method is to have a strong internet presence and establish trust in the selected industry. Affiliates can achieve this by providing high-quality content, engaging with their audience through social media and email marketing, and forming partnerships with other influencers and firms in the field.

Finally, it is crucial to diversify income streams by marketing several products or services from different merchants. This can assist protect against changes in the market or the failure of a particular merchant to pay commissions on time or in whole.

In conclusion, affiliate marketing can be a great source of passive income for individuals who are ready to devote time and resources to growing an audience and establishing their brand in their chosen field. While there are hurdles and risks associated with earning income through affiliate marketing, the potential for high returns and the flexibility of this investment makes it a popular alternative for individuals trying to grow wealth with minimal work. By carefully studying the items or services being pushed, creating a strong online profile, and diversifying revenue sources, affiliates can maximize their returns and attain financial independence through passive income through affiliate marketing.

Peer-to-Peer Lending Income

Peer-to-peer (P2P) lending is an online marketplace that links borrowers and lenders. With P2P lending, individuals can lend money to other individuals or small businesses in exchange for interest payments. This sort of passive income has become increasingly popular in recent years as more people seek alternate investment options with potentially higher returns. This chapter will cover the pros and challenges of earning income through P2P lending and some tactics for maximizing returns.

Advantages of Peer-to-Peer Lending Income

One of the key attractions of P2P lending is the potential for larger returns than traditional savings accounts or CDs. Lenders can often earn interest rates of between 5-10% or more, depending on the borrower's creditworthiness and the duration of the loan period. This can be a steady source of passive income over the long run.

Another benefit of P2P lending is the opportunity to diversify investments among different borrowers and loans. Lenders can invest small amounts in several loans, decreasing their risk to any borrower or investment. This can assist in protecting against default or other risks linked with individual loans.

Difficulties of Peer-to-Peer Lending Income

Notwithstanding the potential benefits of P2P lending, there are also certain drawbacks involved with this sort of passive income. One of the main difficulties is the danger of default. Borrowers may need help to repay the loan, resulting in lost principal and interest for the lender. Lenders must thoroughly analyze the creditworthiness of borrowers and the terms of the loan before investing in reducing this risk.

Another difficulty of P2P lending is the lack of regulation and control. P2P lending platforms are not subject to the same rules as traditional financial institutions, which might increase the risk of fraud or other criminal actions. Lenders must carefully examine the P2P platform and the borrowers before investing to verify that they are respectable and trustworthy.

Ways for Maximizing Returns on P2P Lending Income

Despite the limitations of making revenue through P2P lending, various techniques exist for maximizing returns. One of the most powerful techniques is to carefully examine the borrower's creditworthiness and the terms of the loan before investing. Lenders should evaluate indicators such as the borrower's credit score, income, and debt-to-income ratio to determine the possibility of repayment.

Another key method is to diversify investments over multiple loans and borrowers. This can help lower the risk of default and provide a more reliable source of passive income over the long run. Lenders might consider investing in loans with varied terms and interest rates to establish a balanced portfolio.

Ultimately, it is crucial to analyze investments often and alter tactics as appropriate. Lenders should maintain track of their investments, including the income received and any defaults or late payments. They should also be prepared to adapt their investment plan if market circumstances or other variables change.

In conclusion, P2P lending can be a valuable source of passive income for individuals seeking better yields than traditional savings accounts or CDs. While there are hurdles and hazards associated with earning money through P2P lending, the possibility for better returns and the flexibility to diversify investments make it a popular alternative for investors trying to develop wealth with less effort. By carefully examining the creditworthiness of borrowers, diversifying investments, and checking investments periodically, lenders can maximize their returns and attain financial independence through passive income from P2P lending.

CHAPTER 3

Creating a Portfolio for Passive Income

1. Setting Objectives for Passive Income
2. Finding Your Comfort Level With Risk
3. Choose Which Sources of Passive Income Will Best Suit Your Needs
4. Incorporating Diversification Into Your Investment Strategy
5. Building Several Sources of Passive Income

Setting Objectives for Passive Income

When pursuing financial independence through passive income, it is essential to establish concrete and attainable objectives. The first step in developing a strategy to help you become financially independent is to identify your desired level of passive income. In this chapter, we'll talk about how to establish reasonable expectations for passive income and the steps you may take to make those expectations a reality.

Take Stock of Your Financial Predicament

Assessing your existing financial condition is the first step in deciding what your passive income goals should be. It's important to take stock of your resources, income, and regular outgoings, such as bills and other obligations. To establish how much passive income you need, you must first have a firm grasp of your existing financial condition.

Taking Into Account Personal Preferences

After getting a handle on your financial condition, it's time to think about what you want out of life. Consider the sort of life you hope to lead and the amount of passive income you will need to live that life. Consider things like living costs, food, transportation, and entertainment.

Figure Out How Much Passive Income You Need

You can begin to identify your need for passive income after you have evaluated your current financial condition and identified your lifestyle requirements. This will involve evaluating the amount of passive income you need to cover your living expenditures and attain your financial goals. To figure out how much passive income you need, you can utilize internet calculators or talk to a financial advisor.

Make a Strategy to Realize Your Dream of Passive Income.

After you know how much passive income you want to earn, you can work out a strategy to get there. To do this, you'll need to figure out what kinds of passive income will get you where you want to go and then devise plans to start making more money from those sources.

If you require $5,000 per month in passive income to reach your financial goals, for instance, you'll need to pinpoint the passive income streams that would produce that amount of money. There is a wide variety of investment opportunities available to you, including rental properties, dividend stocks, and peer-to-peer lending websites.

You will also need to design methods for building and growing those income streams over time. This may mean expanding your investment in existing income streams or diversifying your investments to reduce risk and boost profits.

Monitor and Modify Your Plan

Once you have formed a plan to reach your passive income goals, monitoring your progress and altering your plan as needed is crucial. You may need to make modifications to your investing plan or revise your passive income targets if your financial condition or lifestyle needs change over time.

Establishing reasonable and attainable passive income goals is the first step toward building wealth with minimal effort. You can develop a strategy to reach your financial goals by evaluating your current financial standing, thinking about your preferred way of life, and determining your required level of passive income. The key to achieving financial independence and leading the life you want is to plan for and track the steady growth of your passive income streams.

Finding Your Comfort Level With Risk

You should evaluate your comfort level with risk before developing a long-term investment strategy for passive income. The correct passive income streams can be selected for your investment portfolio based on your risk tolerance, which can be determined by evaluating your willingness to take on risk in search of higher returns.

To what extent are you willing to take risks?

A person's risk tolerance indicates how much they can handle in the way of financial unpredictability and variation. It's a gauge of how big of a chance an investor is willing to accept to make a profit. Factors such as a person's age, level of education, career aspirations, and overall financial situation all play a role in shaping their level of risk tolerance.

Finding Your Comfort Level With Risk

Understanding your investment objectives, your financial condition, and your personal preferences are all important factors in determining your risk tolerance. You can determine your level of comfort with risk by following these suggestions.

First, you need to figure out what you hope to accomplish financially through your investments. This could be anything from earning a certain amount of passive income to earning a certain rate of return. Your goals will determine the level of risk you are willing to take on in pursuit of your goals.

Think about your income, expenditures, assets, and liabilities to get a sense of where you are financial. In this way, you can gauge the level of investment risk that is appropriate for your financial situation.

Assess your level of expertise and previous financial experience. You may be more hesitant to take chances and eager to stick to tried-and-true methods of investing if you're just starting. On the other hand, if you have invested before, you could feel more confident taking more chances.

Think about your age and situation: Each of these factors can affect how comfortable you feel taking risks. To protect your retirement funds, for instance, you might be less willing to take chances as you near retirement age. On the other hand, if you're young and have more time to invest, you could feel more comfortable taking more chances.

What Kind of Passive Income Should You Pursue?

Determine your comfort level with risk before deciding which passive income streams are best for your investment portfolio.

Various passive income streams have varied levels of risk and potential returns. Such instances are as follows:

Real estate investing: Real estate investing can offer large potential returns, but also includes higher levels of risk. There are many other types of real estate investments available to investors today, such as rental properties, real estate investment trusts (REITs), and real estate crowdfunding websites.

Dividend-paying stocks: Dividend-paying stocks offer the possibility of steady income streams, but also entail some degree of risk. When deciding which stocks to purchase, investors should think about the company's financial stability and dividend track record.

Profits from peer-to-peer (P2P) lending can be substantial, but the associated risks are also substantial. To reduce their loss exposure, investors should thoroughly assess the creditworthiness of borrowers and spread their money out among several loans.

Low-risk but a low reward: that's what you get with a savings account or certificate of deposit. These investments may be preferred by those who value the safety of the principal more highly than high rates of return.

One of the first things you should do when developing a plan to generate passive income is to evaluate your comfort level with risk. Knowing your risk tolerance, financial status, and investment objectives will help you select your portfolio's best passive income streams. Suppose you want to ensure your investment plan aligns with your preferences and goals. In that case, it's a good idea to examine your risk tolerance and determine if you're more comfortable with high-risk investments that could yield high returns or low-risk ones that could yield lower returns.

Choose Which Sources of Passive Income Will Best Suit Your Needs

If you want to be financially secure in the long run, one of the first things you need to do is construct a robust investment portfolio that includes a variety of passive income streams. Depending on your investment objectives, level of comfort with risk, and other factors, selecting the right passive income stream(s) for you is essential.

While deciding which kind of passive income is best for you, keep the following in mind:

The optimal passive income streams for your portfolio will depend heavily on your financial objectives. Income-oriented assets, like dividend-paying equities, rental properties, or peer-to-peer lending platforms, may be attractive if you're looking to create a steady stream of income. Investments focused on growth, such as crowdsourcing for real estate, equities, or mutual funds, maybe the best choice if you're looking for a way to build your wealth over the long run.

Your risk tolerance indicates the level of danger you are ready to face in exchange for the potential for greater reward. Your choice of passive income streams should be in line with your risk tolerance, as the risk involved with various passive income streams varies. Investments in the form of savings accounts and certificates of deposit (CDs) may appeal to the risk-averse. Higher-risk ventures, such as real estate crowdfunding and peer-to-peer lending, may appeal to you if you have a high tolerance for uncertainty.

The liquidity of an investment is the ease with which it may be turned into cash. Rental properties and real estate crowdfunding, for example, may not be as liquid as dividend stocks or savings accounts. When deciding which forms of passive income to include in your portfolio, you should take your need for liquidity into account.

Diversification: Diversification is a technique that involves spreading your investments over several asset classes, sectors, or businesses. Long-term investors can benefit from diversification by lowering their exposure to risk and increasing their profit potential. To lower your loss exposure and improve your chances of reaching your financial goals, you should think about spreading your passive income streams over other asset classes, such as real estate, stocks, bonds, and P2P lending platforms.

The tax ramifications of passive income may vary depending on the specific passive income stream in question. Examples of taxable income include rental income from real estate and dividends from stocks, which may be subject to capital gains tax. Get in touch with a tax expert to learn how various forms of passive income could affect your overall tax bill.

Instances Where One Can Rely Mostly On Their Income Not Changing

These are some potential sources of passive income and some things to keep in mind when deciding how to allocate your portfolio's resources:

Investing in real estate has a higher standard of risk but also a higher standard of return. There are many other types of real estate investments available to investors today, such as rental properties, real estate investment trusts (REITs), and real estate crowdfunding websites. Think about things like location, property type, and market tendencies when selecting real estate investments.

Stocks that generate dividends can be a stable source of income, but they also come with a measure of

uncertainty. When deciding which stocks to purchase, investors should think about the company's financial stability and dividend track record.

Profits from peer-to-peer (P2P) lending can be substantial, but the associated risks are also substantial. To reduce their loss exposure, investors should thoroughly assess the creditworthiness of borrowers and spread their money out among several loans.

Low-risk but a low reward: that's what you get with a savings account or certificate of deposit. These investments may be preferred by those who value the safety of the principal more highly than high rates of return.

One of the most important aspects of creating lasting wealth is selecting the most suitable passive income streams for your investment portfolio. It is possible to choose passive income streams that fit one's unique circumstances and help one reach one's financial goals by taking into account one's investment goals, risk tolerance, liquidity needs, diversification, and tax consequences. If you're a fan of extreme

Incorporating Diversification Into Your Investment Strategy

Passive income streams are no different from any other type of investment portfolio in that diversification is essential. Risks associated with depending on one form of passive income can be mitigated by investing in many streams. Here, we'll break down why it's so crucial to spread your investments around and offer some advice on how to do just that for your passive income.

For what reasons is it crucial to diversify your portfolio?

With proper diversification, investors can lessen their reliance on any one asset class or source of revenue. When your whole revenue stream depends on a single passive income source and that source suddenly stops working for you, you're in a precarious financial position. You can lessen the likelihood of this happening by increasing your portfolio's diversification. To lessen the risk of having your income fluctuate due to the success or failure of a single asset or source of revenue, diversifying your holdings is essential.

The best way to spread out your source of passive income

Diversifying your portfolio by investing in several types of assets, such as stocks, bonds, and alternative investments, is one strategy. Spreading your investment capital over several various asset classes is a good way to mitigate the impact of any single adverse event.

If you're looking for a way to diversify your portfolio, consider investing in many passive income streams, such as rent, dividends, interest, and royalties. As different forms of passive income provide different rates of return, diversifying your portfolio over multiple passive income streams is a good way to reduce overall investment risk.

If you're going to put money into real estate, spread it around. This is a great way to spread your real estate investments and lower your overall risk.

Invest with a robo-advisor, a service that uses algorithms to create and manage a diversified portfolio of investments tailored to your risk tolerance and financial objectives. Robo-advisors often provide access to numerous investment opportunities in numerous asset classes and income structures.

Keep an eye on your investments to make sure they still reflect your long-term investment objectives and diversification strategy after you've developed a passive income portfolio. If you want to keep your current asset allocation, you may need to rebalance your portfolio from time to time.

Passive income portfolio diversification advantages

Dependence on any one passive income source carries with it a certain amount of risk but spreading that risk around is one of the main benefits of diversification. If you diversify your investments among a variety of income generators and asset types, you can reduce the overall impact of any one investment's failure.

The potential for increased passive income can be achieved through portfolio diversification. Diversifying your investments across multiple revenue streams and asset classes can help you maximize your return while spreading out your risk exposure.

A varied portfolio can help you better align your investments with your long-term financial goals. You can adjust your portfolio's risk and return to fit your comfort level with interest in those factors.

Diversification, in the end, is the key to a prosperous passive income portfolio. To maximize your earnings and minimize your losses, diversify your investment portfolio among a wide range of income sources and asset types. Maintaining a diverse and well-balanced portfolio requires constant attention and adjustments to account for market fluctuations and your changing investing objectives.

Building Several Sources of Passive Income

Although developing multiple sources of passive income may seem like a huge challenge at first, it is essential to reaching your goal of financial independence. Here, we'll go over the measures you may take to initiate your passive income streams and begin making money with little to no effort on your part.

The first stage in establishing passive income streams is to decide what kinds of income streams are appropriate given your investment objectives and level of comfort with risk. Think about the various passive income opportunities, such as rent, dividends, interest, royalties, and affiliate sales.

Once you've settled on a few different sources of passive income, it's time to start researching the many investment opportunities accessible in each. If, for instance, you're hoping to generate rental income, you'll want to investigate the local real estate market and ascertain what kind of property will be the most profitable for your needs.

How much money will be needed? Figure out how much money will be needed to launch each potential source of passive income. The answer to this question is conditional on the nature of your income and the investment opportunity you choose. To earn rent, for instance, you might have to put down money and pay for upkeep on a property, and to earn dividends; you might have to invest in stocks or bonds.

Create a spending plan and a method for bringing in money to supplement your passive income. Think about your budget and how much you can set aside each month for your assets. To attain your goals regarding passive income, you should make some changes to your current budget and financial plan.

You can begin earning passive income through investing once you have determined the sources of passive income you seek, chosen the appropriate investment possibilities, calculated the necessary cash, and established a funding strategy. For example, you could put money into the stock market, a peer-to-peer lending network, or a rental property. Keeping an eye on your investments and making little tweaks as necessary will help you maximize your passive income.

Advice for establishing sources of automatic income

When establishing passive income sources, it's best to take baby steps first. Get started with just one source of revenue, and then add others as you can.

Keep your investments varied to maximize your passive income. Diversify your investments among several different income sources and asset classes to spread out your risk and broaden your earning potential.

It takes time and works to set up passive income streams, so be patient. Having patience and not expecting instant results is crucial.

For help with establishing passive income streams, it's a good idea to consult with financial experts and seasoned investors. You can count on them to offer insightful advice and direction that will bring you closer to your investing objectives.

To sum up, if you want to be financially secure in the future, you need to establish several passive income streams. You'll need to figure out how much money you'll need, create a budget and funding strategy, and start investing to achieve your goals of passive income. By adhering to these guidelines, you may establish a passive income portfolio that serves your needs and is commensurate with the level of risk you are willing to take.

CHAPTER 4

Income from Real Estate Investment

1. How to Pick a Good Investment Property
2. Funding Your Property Purchase
3. Methods for Selecting an Appropriate Property
4. How to Take Care of Your Rental Home
5. Optimizing Your Rental Profits

How to Pick a Good Investment Property

Investing in real estate might produce a sizable passive income. Yet there are many different types of real estate investments, so making the proper decision can take time and effort. Here, we'll go over the various real estate investment opportunities available and help you pick the one that's best for your needs.

For many people, the most appealing aspect of real estate investment is the opportunity to buy a home and then collect rent from renters each month. Apartment buildings, single-family houses, office towers, and retail stores are all examples of real estate. Rental revenue might be reliable, but there is also the responsibility of keeping the property in good repair and running smoothly.

Investing in real estate without actually owning any of the property is possible through real estate investment trusts (REITs). For those unfamiliar, real estate investment trusts (REITs) are businesses that invest in and manage various forms of real estate that generate income for their shareholders. Those who choose to invest in real estate through a REIT can do so by purchasing shares of the company, which entitles them to a portion of the REIT's profits.

Crowdfunding in real estate is a relatively recent investment strategy that facilitates the pooling of capital to invest in real estate projects. This may involve investing in real estate investment trusts (REITs), buying and fixing up existing buildings, or doing all three. Fees for investment management and access to investment possibilities are standard features of crowdfunding platforms.

The term **"flipping"** refers to the practice of buying an undervalued property, making cosmetic improvements, and then selling it for a profit. Renovation and resale of a house for a profit can be a high-risk investment that also offers the potential for big rewards.

Consider your investments, your comfort level with risk, and your current financial condition to select the best real estate investment strategy.

The following are some things to think about while deciding what kind of real estate investment would be best for you:

Considering your investment vestments before deciding on a real estate investment strategy would be best. Real estate investment trusts (REITs) and rental properties can provide stable income. Crowdfunding or flipping houses in the real estate market could be better options if you're searching for steady growth.

Investment risk: Real estate purchases can range from extremely safe to extremely dangerous. It's important to think about how comfortable you are with risk when deciding on a real estate investing strategy. Real estate investment trusts (REITs) and rental homes are safer investments than flipping houses.

Investing in real estate requires careful consideration of one's financial circumstances before settling on the appropriate strategy. Although large sums of money are needed to invest in rental properties and REITs, smaller sums of money may be needed for real estate crowdfunding. It takes a lot of money and skill to "flip" a house or refurbish and sell it for a profit.

Choosing the proper form of real estate investment means taking into account the management requirements. It is common practice for real estate investment trusts (REITs) and real estate crowdfunding platforms to handle management and maintenance duties on behalf of investors so that they can focus on investing. Renovating and selling a property to make a profit is a complex process that demands a lot of time and knowledge.

Finally, **picking the correct form of real estate investment** is crucial to establishing a steady stream of passive income. When deciding what kind of real estate investment is best for you, take into account your investment objectives, level of comfort with risk, available funds, and organizational needs. The right real estate investment, whether in the form of rentals, REITs, crowdfunding, or house flipping, can give both a stable stream of income and the possibility of significant capital appreciation over time.

Funding Your Property Purchase

Although real estate investment has the potential to generate substantial passive income, it also requires a considerable financial commitment. There are a variety of ways to finance your real estate investment and get the ball rolling.

Standard Mortgage

Traditional mortgages are frequently used to fund property investments. To go this route, you would initially put money down on the house and then continue making regular mortgage payments until the debt was repaid. Your mortgage interest rate will be based on several variables or several variables, including your credit history and the state of the mortgage market.

Term Loan With High-Interest Rates

A hard money loan could be a good alternative to a conventional mortgage if you need to close on a property quickly. Private lenders and businesses are the usual sources for loans secured by the collateral value of real estate rather than by the borrower's credit history. Hard money loans are an option for short-term investments despite their higher interest rates compared to conventional mortgages.

Money from the seller

Seller finance is a possible funding source for your next real estate investment. By taking this route, the seller of the property finances the acquisition on behalf of the buyer. If you are having trouble getting a conventional mortgage or want to negotiate more favorable conditions with the seller, this may be a good alternative to explore.

Crowdfunding for Real Estate

Funding real estate investments through crowdfunding platforms is growing in popularity. To implement this strategy, investors pool their resources to finance a property development venture, with each participant ultimately owning a fractional interest in the completed development. If you want to put your money into real estate but want to avoid the hassle of ownership, this may be a good alternative.

Line of Credit Against Equity in One's House

Financing your real estate investment using a home equity line of credit (HELOC) may be an option if you currently own a property. You can finance your investment with a HELOC by borrowing against the equity in your home. Home equity lines of credit (HELOCs) provide competitive interest rates compared to other lending products, but only if you have a substantial amount of equity in your home.

Thinking about your long-term financial objectives and your comfort level with risk might help you decide which financing strategy is best for your real estate investment. It's important to weigh the interest rates, periods, and fees of each choice to ensure you're choosing the most appropriate choice for your budget. A financial advisor or real estate agent can help you sort through the possibilities and make a decision that fits your unique situation.

Methods for Selecting an Appropriate Property

The success of any real estate investment venture hinges on the selection of the correct property. The right investment property helps you achieve your financial objectives while fitting in with your broader plan. To make the most of your real estate investment dollars, consider the following advice:

Establish Your Financial Objectives

Identifying your investment objectives is crucial before beginning your search for a property. Do you want to make a quick buck on a short-term investment, or would you rather invest for the long haul and collect rent payments every month? You can save time and energy by focusing on properties that are a good fit for your investing strategy after you have a firm grasp of what you hope to achieve.

Think About the Spot

One of the most crucial aspects of any real estate investment is its location. In your search for a home to buy, prioritize locations that are in high demand, such as places with reputable schools and convenient public transit. To be sure you're making a good investment, you should also look at the local real estate market and economy.

Inspect the Premises and Report Your Findings

After finding a property in the right area that would yield a profit, it's time to thoroughly analyze the building itself. It's important to think about whether or not the property needs any work done to it. In addition, you should calculate the property's future rental revenue and expenses to make sure they fit within your budget.

Perspectives on the Rivalry

Take into account the local competitors while making a property investment. Compare the characteristics and amenities of your property to those of similar homes now for sale or rent. Learning about the market's current going rate will help you set a fair price that will entice potential tenants or buyers.

Consult a Real Estate Expert.

Finding the right investment property can be difficult but working with a real estate agent can be a huge help. A real estate agent is a useful tool for finding investment homes that fit your criteria and navigating the local market. At every point in the buying procedure, they can offer helpful guidance and insights.

Real estate investments can be a lucrative source of passive income, but only if the right property is purchased. Finding the right property and setting yourself up for long-term financial success requires thinking about your investment goals, evaluating the property, and collaborating with a real estate specialist.

How to Take Care of Your Rental Home

An investment property, once purchased, must be managed well to yield a return. Managing your rental property successfully involves the following steps:

Establish Objectives

Tenant expectations should be spelled out before you rent out your property. Rent, a security deposit, and other lease provisions should all be spelled out. You should also specify who is responsible for what in terms of routine property maintenance and repairs.

Thoroughly Evaluate Potential Tenants

Renting out your property should go well, therefore it's necessary to check out possible tenants first. Checking the tenants' credit and criminal records is one way to verify that they will be responsible and loyal tenants. It would be best if you also interviewed prospective tenants to ensure they are a suitable fit for your property and are aware of the terms of the lease.

Protect the Home and Garden

Keeping up with necessary repairs is crucial to retaining renters. This involves not only keeping the place clean and tidy but also fixing any problems that crop up and adding any new features that may be desirable. Regular upkeep is essential to keep the home in good condition and attract renters.

Be sure you Get Your Rent Money On Time

If you want to keep your rental property lucrative, you need to make sure you collect rent on time every month. Be sure that everyone understands the rent's due date and the consequences of paying late. Think about accepting rent payments online to make life easier for your tenants and increase the likelihood that they'll pay on time.

Be Quick to Address Tenants' Issues

Maintaining good relations with renters requires timely attention to tenant inquiries and problems. Maintain accessibility to address and fix any problems that may occur. By focusing on your tenants' needs and responding quickly to their requests, you may boost the percentage of happy renters and the number of people who rent from you again.

Put your trust in a property manager.

Time and energy are required to manage a rental property, and this burden increases when you have several to look after. If you don't want to deal with the hassle of collecting rent, performing maintenance, and communicating with tenants, you might look into hiring a property manager. Hiring a property manager can free you from day-to-day responsibilities related to managing your investment property, allowing you to concentrate on other elements of your business.

While rental property management isn't a get-rich-quick scheme, it can pay off if you put in the time and effort. Tenants will have a positive experience if you communicate your expectations, keep the property in good condition, and address their issues promptly. If you want to get the most out of your rental property investment, you should probably hire a professional property manager to handle all of the day-to-day operations.

Optimizing Your Rental Profits

To turn your rental property into a lucrative passive income source, you must maximize your rental income.

To maximize your rental income, consider the following:

Fees should go raised.

Raising rent is a simple method to boost rental income. Find out what other people are charging for rent in the neighborhood so you can set a fair one. Consider implementing a slow and steady rent increase for your long-term tenants.

Provide Conveniences

You may be able to charge a higher monthly fee if your rental property has several convenient facilities that tenants appreciate. You might boost your property's desirability by installing high-speed internet, laundry facilities, and fitness centers.

Strengthen the State of Your Property

The condition of your rental property affects how much you can charge in rent. If you make repairs and upgrades, you can charge more. Improvements can be made to the building's aesthetics, such as by repainting or installing new flooring, or to its functionality, by replacing appliances and fixtures.

Rent out parking spots and warehouse space

If your rental property offers spare parking spots or storage areas, you may charge renters a premium to use them. This has the potential to be a lucrative passive income stream that contributes to a higher monthly rental income total.

Accept rent payments online

Tenants' convenience and on-time rent payments can both be increased by accepting payments online. Accepting rent payments online is convenient for both you and your tenants, so think about using a service like PayPal or Venmo.

Fees for Late Payments

To enhance your rental income and encourage tenants to pay on time, consider adding a late fee to their monthly rent. Tenants should be made aware of the late charge policy and its inclusion in the rental agreement.

You need to lower vacancy rates.

To maximize your rental income, it is essential to reduce your vacancy rate. Plan a marketing campaign, such as advertising your rental on rental websites or providing move-in discounts, to entice tenants to rent from you.

Extend Contracts

To keep vacancy rates down and steady rental money coming in, it's a good idea to renew leases with current renters. To encourage lease renewals, you can think about providing renters with rent reductions or upgrading options.

Rental revenue, if managed properly, has the potential to be a lucrative passive income stream. It is possible to enhance rental income and turn a rental property into a profitable investment by raising the rent, providing additional amenities, maintaining and renovating the property, and allowing tenants to pay their rent online. Tenants should be informed of any upcoming policy or price changes well in advance to prevent any confusion.

CHAPTER 5

Earning Passive Income from Stocks and Bonds

1. Stocks and Bonds: Everything You Need to Know
2. Investing Wisely in Stocks and Bonds
3. Investment Portfolio Construction
4. Taking Charge of Your Financial Investments
5. Paying Dividends Back into the Market

Stocks and Bonds: Everything You Need to Know

When it comes to the stock market, two of the most common investment vehicles are stocks and bonds. Making smart choices while assembling a passive income portfolio helps to have a firm grasp of how these instruments function.

Stocks

Stocks represent partial ownership in a corporation. To become a shareholder in a firm and have ownership over a piece of the business, you must first purchase shares. Your stock's value will rise and fall with the ups and downs of the firm and the stock market.

Common stock and preferred stock are the two most frequent kinds of stock.

Unlike preferred equities, which normally yield a variable income, common stocks allow shareholders the power to vote on major corporate decisions.

The value of stocks can change substantially more than the value of bonds over time. On the other hand, they may result in more profits.

Bonds

As a form of debt financing, bonds allow investors to lend money to organizations like corporations and governments. The borrower (business or government) promises to repay the lender (investor) at the end of a predetermined period with interest at a predetermined rate.

In comparison to the fluctuating stock market, the set rate of return offered by bonds is often seen as a safer investment option. But the returns are lower than those from equities.

Generally speaking, bonds can be broken down into two categories: those issued by governments and those issued by corporations. The safest bonds are those issued by governments, which is why governments themselves often issue them. In general, corporate bonds have larger returns than government bonds but also involve a higher degree of risk for the issuing company.

If you want to build a passive income portfolio, you need to know how stocks and bonds differ. Stocks could be a smart investment choice if you're searching for bigger potential profits and can handle a higher degree of risk.

Bonds are a good option if you'd rather have a steady stream of money coming in.

To minimize losses and maximize gains, it is wise to invest in both stocks and bonds. Diversifying your stock and bond portfolio can help you reduce your overall investment risk and boost your returns.

It is not enough to simply know how stocks and bonds differ from one another; you must also be familiar with the measures used to compare them. The P/E ratio, EPS, dividend yield, and bond yield are all examples of such measurements.

Price to earnings, or P/E, is a popular metric for gauging market valuations of publicly traded companies. Investors' strong expectations for a company's future performance might be reflected in a high P/E ratio.

Earnings per share (EPS) is a popular metric used to evaluate business success. It is common knowledge that a more lucrative business will have higher earnings per share.

The dividend yield is calculated by dividing the dividend per share by the stock price per share. For investors, a higher dividend yield may mean a better stock to put their money into.

The return on a bond is measured in terms of its yield. Bonds with a higher yield have a greater opportunity for profit, but they also pose a larger degree of danger.

Acquiring an education in these indicators might aid you in making smart stock and bond investment decisions for your passive income portfolio. You may increase your chances of success and create a sustainable stream of passive income by carefully considering each investment option and by diversifying your portfolio.

Investing Wisely in Stocks and Bonds

Picking the appropriate stocks and bonds is essential if you want to make money off of them passively. There is a plethora of choices and picking the ones that maximize profits with the least amount of risk is no easy feat. If you're looking to build a passive income portfolio with stocks and bonds, here are some things to keep in mind.

You should **first evaluate your investment objectives and level of comfort with risk.** Which do you prefer, growth over the long haul or quick cash? Which of these statements best describes your attitude toward risk: high or low? You can use these criteria to narrow down your options for stocks and bonds.

The next step is to **learn as much as possible about the issuing corporation or organization.** Check their income, margins, and debt-to-equity ratio among other financial metrics. You should also think about any breaking news or events that can affect their future results. In contrast to a company that has recently announced a large lawsuit, one that has just released a new product may have enormous growth potential.

Consider the company's industry and its rivals before investing in its stock. Is it a thriving sector with plenty of opportunity for expansion, or has it reached its natural peak? How does this firm compare to others in terms of market share and new features?

Bond issuer creditworthiness is an important factor to think about. Yet, bonds issued by smaller or lower-rated companies may be riskier than those issued by governments or large, well-respected corporations. Longer-term bonds may provide higher returns, but they also entail more risk, so you should think about when they mature.

Diversification is a critical consideration that should not be overlooked. Spread your investments out over several different firms and industries rather than putting all of your eggs in one basket. One way to do this is by the purchase of a share of a mutual fund or exchange-traded fund (ETF) that has a diversified portfolio of equities and bonds.

Pay attention to both the fees and the track record of a fund's or ETF's performance when making a selection. Low performance may be an indication of bad management, while high fees might chip away at your profits. Try to find funds that have both a good return record and reasonable costs.

Last but not least, **keep in mind that the stock and bond markets can be unpredictable.** The economy, firm success, and international politics are just a few of the elements that might affect prices. Investing should be done with a long-term horizon in mind, rather than reacting emotionally to daily fluctuations in the market.

To sum up, it is important to think about your investment objectives and level of risk tolerance, estimate the issuer's financials and industry, diversify your holdings, and keep fees and past performance in mind when selecting stocks and bonds for your passive income portfolio. Building a passive income-generating stock and bond portfolio takes time, but it is possible with careful planning and a long-term investment horizon.

Investment Portfolio Construction

Anybody seeking to generate passive income from stocks and bonds should **prioritize building a diversified investment portfolio.** A diverse portfolio spreads your assets out so that your money isn't all riding on the success of one company or industry. Important factors to think about when constructing a diverse investment portfolio are as follows:

Asset allocation is crucial in assembling a diverse investment strategy. During investing, asset allocation refers to the act of allocating your portfolio among various asset classes including stocks, bonds, and cash based on your investment objectives, risk tolerance, and time horizon. Investing in a way that strikes a good balance between risk and return will bring you closer to your financial goals.

Investing across multiple sectors helps create a more robust portfolio. This entails putting money into businesses across a wide range of sectors, including healthcare, tech, and consumer goods. One's risk of loss due to the volatility and unpredictability of any given industry is mitigated by this.

Investing in businesses located in different parts of the world is yet another strategy to spread the risk throughout your portfolio. This strategy entails putting money into businesses in both the domestic and international markets, spreading investment risk across a variety of economies and regulatory environments. Growth potential in emerging markets is just one more reason to diversify internationally.

It is crucial to **strike a balance between risk and reward while constructing a diverse investment portfolio**. This entails putting money into both high-risk, high-return assets like equities and low-risk, low-return bonds. Your investment objectives and level of comfort with risk will determine the relative size of your allocation to various asset classes.

After you have a diversified investment portfolio set up, you should **rebalance it regularly** to keep your holdings in the proportions you choose. During a rebalance, you sell some assets and buy others to get your portfolio back to its initial asset allocation. By doing so, you can keep your portfolio well-balanced and on track with your long-term financial objectives.

One of the most important steps in developing a passive income stream from stocks and bonds is to construct a diversified investment portfolio. Investors can lower their overall exposure to risk and improve their chances of meeting their long-term investing objectives by diversifying over a wide range of assets, industries, and locations. Keeping your portfolio in line with your investment goals can also be aided by routine monitoring and rebalancing.

Taking Charge of Your Financial Investments

The next stage, after constructing a diverse investment portfolio suitable for your passive income objectives and level of risk appetite, is to manage it prudently. For optimal returns on your investments, consider the following advice:

Keep a close eye on your investments frequently to make sure they're doing well. Maintaining a regular monitoring schedule will allow you to spot problems quickly so you can fix them. When you keep an eye on your portfolio consistently, you can make adjustments based on the latest market information.

If you want to keep your portfolio from becoming unbalanced, you should rebalance it regularly. Your investment portfolio may become unbalanced as a result of this. It is crucial to rebalancing your portfolio regularly to keep your asset allocation and risk level where you want them to be. To keep your portfolio balanced, you may need to sell off some winning investments and replace them with losing ones.

You should **spread your money around to reduce your risk.** Spreading your investments over several asset categories and industries will help you weather market fluctuations more comfortably. Contrary to popular belief, diversification does not necessitate investing in every market or asset class. Instead, you should spread your money around among assets that work well together.

Fees should be monitored closely since they have the potential to erode investment results. To get the most out of your investments, you should monitor your fees and seek out ways to minimize them. To reduce your investment costs, you might, for instance, choose exchange-traded funds (ETFs) or index funds (funds) over actively managed funds.

One of the most common mistakes investors make is letting their feelings influence their choice of investments. Impulsive choices driven by greed or fear might hurt your investment portfolio. If you want to succeed in the long run, you need to stick to your investment strategy.

Keep up with the tax consequences, as they can have a major bearing on your investment returns if you're not prepared. You should always be aware of the tax ramifications of your investments and work to reduce your tax burden. You can invest in tax-deferred accounts like

IRAs and 401(k)s and take advantage of tax-loss harvesting to reduce your taxable income.

Last but not least, maintain your self-control and stick to your investment strategy. Don't let short-term fluctuations in the market cause you to abandon your long-term investment strategy. Keep in mind that investing is a long-term strategy, and that patience and self-control are essential to your success.

In conclusion, generating passive income streams requires careful management of your investment portfolio. You can maximize your returns and attain your passive income goals through regular monitoring of your assets, rebalancing your portfolio, diversifying your investments, watching fees, avoiding emotional judgments, staying up to current on tax consequences, and practicing discipline.

Paying Dividends Back into the Market

While accumulating wealth through dividends from stocks and bonds, it is essential to reinvest dividends. The term "dividend reinvestment" refers to the practice of buying more shares of a company's stock or a bond issuer's bond using the money you receive as a shareholder. The result is the exponential growth of your money due to compounding.

Consider these arguments in favor of reinvesting your dividends:

Your dividends compound, meaning that the interest you earn on them grows over time as you reinvest them. Because of this, your investment may grow exponentially over time due to compounding returns. The profits you receive are proportional to the amount you reinvest.

It is cost-effective to reinvest dividends since most corporations have dividend reinvestment programs (DRIPs) that allow you to do so without paying any transaction costs. The profits you get can be reinvested tax-free, increasing your potential return.

Reinvesting dividends is an example of automatic investing, in which you don't have to make any decisions about your investments or actively manage your portfolio. Without worrying about short-term fluctuations or making rash decisions, you may maintain your investment strategy and keep your eye on the prize of reaching your long-term goals.

Rewards Over Time: Reinvesting dividends is a long-term approach that can help you amass substantial money. You can speed up your progress toward financial independence by reinvesting dividends. When you reinvest your dividends, you buy more shares and increase your income stream independently of the stock market's performance.

There are, however, a few things to keep in mind when deciding how to reinvest your dividends:

Although dividends that are reinvested do not appear on a shareholder's cash statement, they are nevertheless subject to taxation. The dividend income you receive, even if reinvested, will still be subject to taxation. If you want to know how your dividends will be taxed if you reinvest them, you should talk to a tax expert.

If you reinvest your dividends, you are increasing the total number of shares outstanding and, thus, reducing your percentage ownership. Because of this, the value of your shares may decline (a phenomenon known as "dilution"). Yet this is something to think about in the far future, and it may not have much of an immediate effect on your investment performance.

Over-concentration in a single investment can occur if dividends are reinvested in the same stock or bond. Diversification is the solution. It can make your portfolio less diversified and raise your risk level. Investing in numerous stocks and bonds can help spread out your risk and increase your returns.

In conclusion, if you want to grow your dividend-based wealth, you should reinvest your dividends. It's easy to set up, doesn't cost much, and has the potential to generate high profits because of compounding. But, while deciding how to reinvest your dividends, it is important to keep the following in mind to get the most out of your money while limiting your risk: taxes, dilution, and lack of diversity.

CHAPTER 6

Generating Passive Income from IP

1. Legal Aspects of Intellectual Property
2. Putting Pen to Paper (or Screen) for Books, Digital Editions, and Audiobooks
3. Making and Marketing Digital Courses
4. Software Development and Distribution
5. Everything You Need to Know About Selling Your Recordings, Paintings, and Photos Under a License

Legal Aspects of Intellectual Property

One of the most profitable and potentially satisfying forms of passive income is royalties obtained through intellectual property. Learn more about intellectual property and how you can use it to generate a residual income in this chapter.

Inventions, works of literature and art, logos, company names, and brand identities are all examples of intellectual property. Trade secrets, patents, and trademarks are all forms of intellectual property protection. Inventions, logos, software, and works of literature are all examples of intellectual property.

Royalties are the most typical kind of passive income derived from IP. As compensation for the use or exploitation of intellectual property, royalties are paid to the original creator. Royalties are monetary compensation for the use of an author's or musician's intellectual property, such as a song or book.

Depending on the type of intellectual property you own, you may be entitled to royalties that provide a steady stream of passive income. Patents, copyrights, and trademarks are the most typical.

Protecting new ideas and discoveries through the law is what patents do. They grant the patent holder the monopoly to produce, utilize, and sell the patented invention for a specified time frame. Anyone, not the patent holder who wants to use the innovation must first get permission from or pay a licensing fee to the inventor. The patent holder may then receive periodic royalties as a result.

Authoritative works like books, songs, and movies are safeguarded by copyrights. Owners of copyrights are granted the sole privilege of duplicating, distributing, and exhibiting the protected work. The right to use a copyrighted work belongs to the copyright owner, and anybody who wishes to use it must either get permission from the owner or pay a licensing fee.

Companies use trademarks, which can be anything from a logo to a catchy slogan, to identify their products and services from those of competitors. The owner of a trademark might make a passive income by licensing the use of the trademark in connection with goods and services to third parties.

Earning passive income from intellectual property has many advantages, one of which is that you don't have to be hands-on in managing your IP to make money from it. After completing your innovation or literary work, you can relax and wait for the royalties to arrive. It's worth noting, nevertheless, that developing original IP often calls for substantial outlays of resources.

Earning a living off of IP might be beneficial because it can give a steady flow of money for years to come. After granting a license for your IP, you will be entitled to ongoing royalty payments for the duration of the license's term.

Earning a living off of intellectual property does not come without some possible pitfalls, though. Defending your ideas from copycats is a difficult task. In today's digital world, where it's simple for others to reproduce and distribute your work without your permission, this can be very challenging.

Nevertheless, intellectual property is often subject to intense rivalry in the marketplace. Because of this, it may be challenging to find a licensee who is ready to pay a high enough royalty rate to justify the costs of developing the IP.

Understanding the legal protections available to you and the market demand for your intellectual property is crucial to your success in earning a passive income from royalties on intellectual property. If you want your intellectual property to be seen by potential licensees, you may need to spend money on marketing and promotion.

Finally, intellectual property royalties can be a highly lucrative and satisfying form of passive income. It enables you to generate revenue with minimal management effort and has the potential to do so for the duration of the license agreement. Nonetheless, one must be prepared for difficulties and have a thorough knowledge of legal safeguards and market conditions.

Putting Pen to Paper (or Screen) for Books, Digital Editions, and Audiobooks

One effective strategy to make passive income from intellectual property is to write and publish books, e-books, and audiobooks. It may take a lot of time and energy upfront to write a book, but once it's published, it can bring in money for years to come, regardless of whether the book is fiction, nonfiction, or a how-to guide.

Book authors should first consider whether or not their target audience is interested in their potential subject matter. Be sure there will be demand for the book by doing market research and locating a specific audience. Having settled on a subject, the next step is to plan out the paper and get started writing.

Once the manuscript is complete, the author has numerous publishing routes to choose from. Finding an agency and publishing house to take care of your book's editing, printing, and distribution is essential for traditional publication. Yet, when you self-publish, you're responsible for everything from editing to marketing. The proliferation of e-books and print-on-demand services has contributed to self-meteoric publishing's surge in popularity in recent years.

Hybrid publishing incorporates features of both traditional and self-publishing. In hybrid publishing, the author collaborates with a company that handles editorial, design, and distribution, but maintains a greater say over the project and its financial outcomes.

There are many avenues open to the author after the book has been released. Payment through royalties is a typical practice. Once a book is sold, the author receives a royalty payment equal to a specified percentage of the book's retail price. The publishing approach and the terms of the contract can affect the royalty percentage.

Licensing is another source of revenue. To license something is to grant permission, in exchange for payment, for another party to use your intellectual property. An author may choose to grant a film or television production company the right to adapt his or her work.

Recent years have seen a meteoric rise in the sales of electronic books, which have many benefits for authors. To make up for the lower cost of production, electronic books are often priced lower. Electronic books have the added benefits of global distribution and simple revision and update.

Audiobooks are another option for authors looking to generate passive income. Audiobooks have become increasingly popular in recent years due to the rise of audiobook platforms like Audible. Creating an audiobook involves recording the book in a studio or hiring a narrator to record it for you. Once the audiobook is produced, it can be sold on platforms like Audible, and the author can receive royalties each time it is sold.

In addition to generating income from book sales, authors can also earn money through speaking engagements and merchandise sales. Speaking engagements can be a great way to promote the book and generate additional income. Merchandise sales, such as t-shirts or other items featuring the book's cover or characters, can also be a way to generate additional income.

Creating and publishing books, e-books, and audiobooks can be a lucrative way to generate passive income from intellectual property. While it can take a lot of time and effort upfront, once the book is published, it can generate income for years to come. By understanding the publishing options and finding the right niche, authors can create a successful stream of passive income.

Making and Marketing Digital Courses

Developing and selling online courses is a popular way to generate passive income. With the growing demand for online education, creating an online course has become easier than ever.

In this section, we will discuss the steps involved in developing and selling online courses.

Choose your topic: The first step in creating an online course is to choose a topic that you are knowledgeable about and passionate about. The topic should also be in demand and have the potential to attract a large audience. You can choose to create a course on a technical subject, a hobby or skill, or a topic related to personal development.

Identify your target audience: Once you have chosen your topic, you need to identify your target audience. This will help you to tailor your course to meet the needs of your audience. You can use online tools such as Google Analytics to gather data on your target audience's demographics and interests.

Create your course content: The next step is to create your course content. You can use a variety of media such as videos, audio, slides, and text to create your course. Your course should be engaging, informative, and easy to follow. You can also include quizzes, assignments, and assessments to ensure that your students are actively engaged in the learning process.

Choose your platform: Once your course content is ready, you need to choose a platform to host and sell your courses. Several online courses platforms such as Udemy, Coursera, and Teachable allow you to create and sell courses. You can also choose to host your course on your website.

Price your course: Pricing your course is an important decision that can impact your sales. You need to find the right balance between affordability and profitability. You can research the pricing of similar courses in your niche to get an idea of the market price. You can also offer discounts and promotions to attract more students.

Market your course: Marketing your course is crucial to its success. You can use social media, email marketing, and content marketing to promote your course. You can also collaborate with influencers and bloggers in your niche to reach a wider audience.

Provide customer support: Once you have sold your course, you need to provide customer support to your students. This includes answering questions, providing feedback, and resolving technical issues. Providing excellent customer support can lead to positive reviews and referrals.

In conclusion, developing and selling online courses is a great way to generate passive income. With the right approach and strategy, you can create a course that meets the needs of your audience and generates revenue for years to come.

Software Development and Distribution

Creating and licensing software is one of the most lucrative ways to generate passive income through intellectual property. This form of passive income can be achieved by developing software applications and licensing them for a fee. Software licensing is the process of selling the rights to use a software program to others. In this chapter, we will discuss how to create and license software for passive income.

Developing Software

Developing software can be a complex and time-consuming process, but it can also be very rewarding. The first step in creating software is to identify a need or a problem that the software can solve. Once you have identified the need, you can start planning and designing your software. This involves creating a detailed specification of the software, including the features and functionalities it will have.

Next, you will need to choose the programming language and tools you will use to develop the software. You may also need to hire a software developer or a team of developers to help you with the development process.

When developing software, it is important to keep in mind the end-users and ensure that the software is user-friendly, efficient, and meets their needs. The software should be tested thoroughly to ensure that it works as intended and is free of bugs and glitches.

The Process of Purchasing Software Licenses

When you're ready to start making money off of your program, licensing is the next step. Selling licenses to use the software commercially is called licensing.

The software can be licensed in one of two main ways: either under a proprietary model or under an open-source model.

Authorization to Use Someone Else's Intellectual Property

Purchasing a proprietary license grants the buyer the only right to run the software. Because of copyright protections, the owner of proprietary software has sole authority over its reproduction, resale, and alteration. As the owner of the program, you can earn greatly from proprietary licensing since you can charge a high price for the license to use your product.

Permission less Distribution

But under open-source licensing, the program's source code is made freely available to everyone. If the licensing terms are followed, then the program can be used, modified, and distributed by anybody. Although open-source licensing does not directly result in monetary gain, it has the potential to be employed as a promotional tool for other goods and services.

How to Promote and Sell Your Software

The next step after creating and obtaining a license for your program is to promote and sell it.

Among the many methods for promoting and selling software are:

Where to sell your software online:
There are many online markets where you may sell your software, such as the Apple App Store and the Google Play Store.

Also, you can use **affiliate marketing** to spread the word and generate sales for your program. With affiliate marketing, other websites or businesses can help advertise your app in exchange for a cut of the profits.

Email marketing, social media marketing, and other types of digital marketing are all examples of direct marketing that may be used to reach out to potential buyers for your product.

The term **"bundling"** refers to the practice of selling your software alongside other related software or services.

Programming Administration

It is crucial to properly manage your software once it has been licensed and sold so that it may continue to bring in revenue even after your involvement has ended. This entails maintaining compatibility with new OSes and hardware, distributing updates and bug patches, and responding to consumer inquiries.

Making money off of intellectual property can be difficult but creating and licensing software can be a very lucrative method to do so. However, high-quality software that caters to your client's requirements calls for a substantial investment of time and resources. When you follow the advice in this chapter, you can develop and license software that brings in residual income for years to come.

Everything You Need to Know About Selling Your Recordings, Paintings, and Photos Under a License

Detailed Information on Licensing Your Creative Works for Financial Gain

Licensing your creative works, such as music, artwork, or photography, is a great way to earn passive money that is often overlooked. Artists and photographers who are trying to monetize their work may find licensing to be an interesting option because it can give a regular source of passive money without the need for continual effort.

You can license your creative work if you want to see it used in a commercial context like a website or ad campaign. A licensing agreement normally specifies the allowed uses, the agreed-upon payment, and the length of time for the license.

Artists and photographers can license their work and generate residual money by taking advantage of the following opportunities:

Online libraries of stock images have become a commonplace method of commercializing digital paintings, pictures, and other forms of visual art. Accessing and downloading high-resolution photographs from these sites is a breeze. If you're a photographer or artist, you may use these sites to share your work and get paid for each download or license sale. Shutterstock, iStock, and Getty Images are just a few of the many prominent stock photo and artwork websites.

Artists and photographers can also offer commercial usage licenses for their creations. Using works of art or pictures for commercial or branding purposes falls under this category. Licenses for commercial usage can be lucrative because they sometimes need a bigger initial payment and may continue indefinitely. Negotiating the conditions of the license and drafting a licensing contract with the customer are standard practices when licensing your work for commercial use.

Reproductions of original works of art known as "fine art prints" can be licensed by artists. Artist proofs, open editions, and limited editions are all viable distribution models for fine art prints. Collaboration with a printmaker who can reproduce and sell your artwork is essential when licensing your work for fine art prints. The artist retains ownership of the original piece while the printmaker keeps a cut of the profits.

When you license your artwork or images for merchandising, you're essentially permitting them to be printed on a wide variety of items, from T-shirts to mugs to phone covers. Merchandising contracts are frequently long-term commitments that may include a sales-based royalty payment. As popular designs may be sold in huge quantities, merchandising can be a valuable source of passive income.

For usage in films, TV shows, or documentaries, you must first obtain a license to do so. In the film and television industries, licensing costs can add up quickly, especially for well-known or widely-viewed works.

Finally, you can earn money without consistently working at it by licensing your creative works such as music, art, or photography. To figure out how to best commercialize their creations, artists, and photographers should investigate available licensing options and distribution channels. Copyright law and license conditions are complex and should be thoroughly understood before engaging in any licensing agreements.

CHAPTER 7

Affiliate Marketing as a Source of Passive Income

1. Learning About Affiliate Programs
2. A Guide to Choose the Best Affiliate Programs
3. Producing High-Quality Material for Advertising Purposes
4. Building and Expanding Your Fanbase
5. Keeping Tabs on the Outcomes of Your Affiliate Marketing Efforts

The Basics of Affiliate Marketing

Affiliate marketing is a form of pay-for-performance advertising in which an individual or business is financially rewarded for generating sales of another firm's goods or services. This method of making passive income online is gaining popularity.

Affiliate marketing is based on the mutually beneficial relationships between the seller (or merchant), the affiliate (or middleman), and the buyer (or consumer). Affiliates drive traffic to the merchant's site by recommending it to their followers, who make purchases. Commissions paid to affiliates are often a certain proportion of the sale price.

Affiliate marketing's low entry barrier is one of its primary benefits. To become an affiliate marketer, you must create a website or social media account to sell products, unlike founding a business or investing in real estate.

The fact that it can be adapted to different situations is another perk. Affiliates have complete autonomy in deciding which items and promotional strategies to implement. As long as they have access to the internet, they can do their jobs from any location.

Although there are many benefits to affiliate marketing, it has its challenges. The possibility of fraud is a major concern. Some affiliates may spam customers or advertise scam products to maximize their earnings. The retailer's and the industry's reputations may suffer due to this.

The market is always changing, so staying flexible is another obstacle. To maintain commissions, affiliates must keep up with the latest trends in consumer preferences for products and services.

Many people have found success with affiliate marketing despite these obstacles. Promoting one of the many available niches and products can generate passive income with the right approach and strategy.

Affiliate marketing is a competitive field; you must know the ropes to succeed. This encompasses a wide range of affiliates and merchandising payment structures.

Affiliates can be divided into three categories:

- Content creators
- Influencers
- Coupon and deal sites.

Bloggers and YouTubers create content for their audiences based on a specific topic or niche, and they often advertise related products. Yet, influencers can push products to their enormous online communities because of their extensive online followings. Websites that offer coupons and deals encourage consumers to buy by providing steep price cuts and limited-time specials.

Affiliates can be paid in several different ways by merchants. Sales commissions often expressed as a percentage of the transaction price, are the most prevalent. In addition, some vendors pay affiliates a certain amount per referral for every click on their affiliate link.

Picking the correct items to advertise is crucial to your affiliate marketing success. That's why it's so important to zero in on offerings that both interest your target market and tend to result in sales. It would help if you only advertised things you truly believe in and be honest with your audience about being an affiliate marketer.

In general, affiliate marketing is a promising method to generate passive revenue through the World Wide Web. But you need to go into it with the appropriate mindset and know what to expect in terms of obstacles and risks.

A Guide to Choose the Best Affiliate Programs

Affiliate marketing has quickly become one of the most popular methods of earning extra money in your spare time. Affiliate marketing entails promoting services or goods from third parties in exchange for a commission on sales via your referral link. Affiliate marketing is appealing because you can start making money right away without spending any money by promoting things you already believe in and using yourself.

Finding the correct affiliate program is a crucial first step in affiliate marketing. Choose wisely from the many affiliate programs out there; doing so can significantly impact your business. You can discover some helpful hints below if you're looking for an affiliate program.

Find Your Target Market Through Investigation.

Affiliate marketing is a great way to make money online, but you should find your specialty before you go in. A person's niche is their area of expertise and personal interest. If health and wellness is an area that interests you, you may promote related products. You can use this strategy to find affiliate programs that are a good fit for your specialty.

Look into the Organization of the Commission

The affiliate program's commission structure is a major element to think about. It is important to select an affiliate program with a competitive commission rate, as commission rates differ across programs. Depending on the item and the scheme, the affiliate commission could be anywhere from 5% to 50%.

Think About the Store's Reputation Before You Buy

When deciding on an affiliate program, assessing the retailer's credibility is important. It's crucial to do business with reliable vendors who provide high-quality goods. If you follow these steps, you may rest assured that the things you're selling are authentic and of great quality.

Analyze the Promotional Resources Made Available

The availability of helpful marketing resources and customer service is also crucial when selecting an affiliate network. Some affiliate programs may provide banners, links, and other promotional materials to assist you in promoting their products. Having access to helpful customer service in the event of questions or problems is another crucial feature to look for in software.

Keep an Eye Out for Prospects That Will Pay Off Down the Road

It's important to search for sustainable growth when selecting an affiliate program. Choose a program with high customer lifetime value or recurring commissions to achieve this. This will guarantee a steady flow of passive revenue long after the first sale.

In conclusion, if you want to be successful in affiliate marketing, you need to pick the correct affiliate program. You can find an affiliate program that fits your needs and helps you earn a substantial passive income by researching your niche, checking the commission structure, thinking about the merchant's reputation, reviewing the marketing tools and support provided, and looking for long-term opportunities.

Producing High-Quality Material for Advertising Purposes

One way to generate money online with little work is through affiliate marketing. Unfortunately, affiliate marketing success requires more than just recommending products. Also, you'll want to promote your products effectively by writing engaging content that draws in your ideal customers. Here we'll talk about several ways to improve your product promotion content.

Learning about your intended readers is the first step in writing effective content. Who are they, exactly? Just what are their passions, exactly? Just what issues are they facing that your affiliate products can remedy? To achieve your goals, you must first identify and learn about your audience so that you can tailor your material to them.

Telltales; anecdotes are far more memorable than cold hard data when trying to get a message through. Telling a narrative is a great way to get your point across and draw attention to the positive aspects of your selling. Recount times when you've profited from using the product yourself, or the times when you've heard other people describe using it.

Your content should be useful to your readers. Please provide them with facts they can use to determine whether or not to purchase your endorsed products. Give them advice on how to maximize the use of the things they purchase.

Be trustworthy: Integrity is of the utmost importance in the affiliate marketing industry. Always be honest about what you're selling and how much money you're making. Don't mislead customers by making inflated claims about the products. Give your readers an honest assessment of the product's merits and draw their conclusions.

Incorporate multimedia elements into your content. These could include text, images, videos, and infographics. It's a nice way to break up the text and keep the reader interested. Promote your wares in style by including high-resolution photos and videos that show off their features and functionality.

Employ Search Engine Optimization (SEO): If you want your material to perform well in search engines, you need to create it with SEO in mind. Make it easy for your intended audience to find your material by using keywords associated with your promoting products.

Make good use of social media to spread the word about your affiliate links and increase site traffic. To increase your audience's trust and respect for you, you should publish material on social media and interact with them.

Maintain regularity: Regularity is a must in affiliate marketing. Maintaining your audience's interest and engagement requires consistently creating and publishing high-quality content. To ensure that you consistently offer your audience value, create a content calendar and stick to it.

The ability to **consistently provide high-quality content** is crucial to any affiliate marketing program's long-term viability. You may generate content that interests your audience and promotes the things you're selling if you research your demographic, use narrative, provide value, are honest, employ multimedia, search engine optimization, and social media, and remain consistent. Don't forget that the secret to affiliate marketing success is to earn your audience's trust and respect by consistently delivering on their expectations.

Building and Expanding Your Fanbase

Earning money with little to no effort is possible thanks to affiliate marketing's potential for passive income. Making money as an affiliate means marketing products or services and receiving a cut of any sales made as a result of your promotion. Nevertheless, if you want to make a decent living from affiliate marketing, you need to put your attention where it counts: on expanding your audience. If you're an affiliate marketer, here are several ways to expand your clientele:

Think Carefully About Your Target Market and Offerings

Affiliate marketers should start by carefully selecting their target market and the products they will promote. You need to zero in on a certain subset of consumers and pick out products that are both in line with your niche and relevant to the interests of that subset. It's important to promote things that you have faith in and that you'd buy for yourself if given the chance.

Think of Useful Material to Produce

To attract a larger following and expand your current one, you must produce high-quality material. Your content's worth lies in the problem it solves or the objective it advances. Content like this might be in the form of reviews, tutorials, how-to guides, and anything else that provides useful information to your target audience and helps them learn more about your product.

Construct a Website or Blog.

The cornerstone of any successful affiliate marketing campaign is a website or blog. You'll use it to share your work with the world and advertise your affiliate links. Your website must be both aesthetically pleasing and functional for your target audience and search engines. You'll see a boost in your search engine rankings and site traffic as a result.

Make use of networking sites

To expand and engage with your current audience, social media is crucial. Social media sites like Facebook, Twitter, Instagram, and LinkedIn provide excellent opportunities to disseminate information about your content and affiliate links, interact with your target audience, and expand your online presence generally. Selecting the best social media channels for your niche and intended audience and developing a plan for using them is essential for effective affiliate marketing.

Accumulate a mailing list.

One efficient strategy for expanding your viewership is to start an email list. Promote your content and affiliate links, connect with your audience, and increase website traffic through email marketing. In exchange for people's email addresses, you should provide them with something of value, like a free eBook or newsletter.

Communicate With Your Target Market

It's essential to interact with your audience if you want to gain their loyalty and a larger following. It would be best if you were quick to respond to messages and comments, open to suggestions, and eager to have your readers spread the word about your work. To be successful as an affiliate marketer, you need to earn the confidence and credibility of your target audience.

Keep an eye on your KPIs and make adjustments as needed.

As an affiliate marketer, your audience size and growth depend on how closely you monitor your data and adapt your plan. To evaluate the success of your plan, monitor metrics like website visits, social media shares, email open and click rates, and affiliate revenue. Use this information to figure out what is working and what isn't, and then alter your approach accordingly.

In conclusion, creating and expanding your audience is essential if you want to succeed as an affiliate marketer. Affiliate marketing may be a lucrative business if you put in the time and effort to find the right niche and products, write helpful content, set up a website or blog, leverage social media, compile an email list, interact with your audience, and track your KPIs.

Keeping Tabs on the Outcomes of Your Affiliate Marketing Efforts

Affiliate marketing can be a valuable source of passive income with no effort and financial outlay. But just like any other enterprise, it calls for planning and hard work to succeed. Here we'll talk about how monitoring and analyzing your affiliate marketing data might help you make more money in the future.

You may learn what kinds of products and promotional strategies are most successful by keeping tabs on your affiliate marketing data. In addition, it aids in revealing problem areas so that you can make necessary adjustments to your approach. Analytics tools may help you keep tabs on how well your website or social media pages are performing, which is the first step in keeping a close eye on your results.

Google Analytics is a robust program that may teach you a lot about your website's visitors and their habits. It lets you monitor things like visitors' behaviors (such as page views, clicks, and purchases) on your site. In addition to monitoring your site's traffic, Google Analytics can keep tabs on your affiliate links, revealing which products are drawing in the most interest and which links are getting the most clicks.

Bitly is another tool that may be used to monitor the effectiveness of affiliate marketing. Using Bitly, you can shorten your links and monitor their click-through rates. In this way, you can assess the performance of your advertising initiatives and alter them as necessary.

You can start analyzing your affiliate marketing results when you have enough information. Indicators like these should not be ignored.

The conversion rate is the proportion of site visitors who go on to purchase after clicking one of your affiliate links. If your conversion rate is low, it could be because your advertising needs to reach its target audience.

The percentage of site visitors who click on one of your affiliate links is known as the "click-through rate" (CTR). If your

CTR is poor, it could be because your marketing content is boring or irrelevant.

The average amount of money you make per sale made through your affiliate links is known as the "average order value" (AOV). Raising your average order value (AOV) can boost your revenue significantly, even without a rise in site visitors.

When you know what needs fixing, you can start trying out alternative approaches to marketing to discover what resonates with your target demographic. To find out what kind of content gets the most attention and ultimately leads to sales, you may, for instance, experiment by writing product reviews and how-to instructions.

You should also check in on your affiliates and make sure they're still relevant every once in a while. Certain collaborations may no longer be useful as your target audience and advertising techniques develop. By evaluating your affiliate relationships regularly, you may promote high-quality goods to your target audience while earning lucrative commissions.

It is essential to monitor your affiliate marketing performance while also keeping up with the latest developments and best practices in the field. Doing so can help you get ahead of the competition and find fresh avenues for expansion. Taking part in online discussion groups and attending conferences might help you learn more about your field and meet other professionals.

To sum up, if you want to make the most money possible from your affiliate marketing efforts, you need to measure and analyze the results. You may improve your affiliate marketing efforts by keeping an eye on key indicators and trying out new approaches to promotion. Being abreast of developments and best practices in your field can also help you keep pace with the competition and spot emerging markets. Affiliate marketing has the potential to be a significant passive revenue stream with the appropriate strategy and dedication to continuous growth.

CHAPTER 8

Earning Money While You Sleep: Peer-to-Peer Lending

1. Learning About P2P Loans
2. Methods for Deciding on a Reliable Online Lending Service
3. Criteria for Judging Loans and Borrowers
4. Taking Charge of Your Loan Portfolio
5. Profitability while limiting exposure to lose.

Learning About P2P Loans

Crowdlending, which is another name for peer-to-peer (P2P) lending, has emerged as a popular way to earn passive income in recent years. By using peer-to-peer (P2P) lending systems, investors can lend money directly to borrowers, cutting out intermediaries like banks.

Using peer-to-peer (P2P) lending, investors can pool their funds to provide loans to borrowers. P2P lending systems allow borrowers to apply for loans and then use an internal algorithm to determine the applicant's creditworthiness and risk level. Lending money to borrowers is an option for investors who want to finance businesses or individuals based on their own risk appetite and financial objectives.

P2P lending has a lot going for it, and one of the best parts is the possibility for high returns in comparison to more conventional passive income sources like savings accounts and CDs. Investors might potentially earn larger returns with P2P lending platforms because their interest rates are higher than those offered by conventional banks.

Diversifying assets over several different borrowers and loan kinds is another benefit of P2P lending. Personal loans, business loans, and mortgage loans are just some of the loan options that are generally made available through P2P lending platforms. Investors can reduce their exposure to default risk and potential loss by diversifying their loan portfolios across numerous categories.

Despite the benefits of peer-to-peer lending, there are drawbacks and risks that investors should be aware of. The possibility of borrower defaults is a major threat. Although if P2P lending platforms utilize algorithms to determine a borrower's trustworthiness, there is still the possibility of loan default and consequent investor losses.

Lack of cash is another threat associated with P2P lending. As P2P loans are not as liquid as traditional investments like stocks or bonds, investors may have difficulty promptly withdrawing their money if they need to do so.

In addition, the FDIC does not insure P2P lending platforms, therefore investors' funds are at risk in the case of a platform failure.

Investors that are exploring P2P lending as a source of passive income should conduct extensive research about the platforms they are investigating. Investors should prioritize platforms with a proven history of successful loan repayments and a solid reputation for honesty and integrity in the industry.

When deciding on P2P loans to invest in, investors need also think about their risk tolerance and financial goals. There is a tradeoff between the potential reward from a higher-risk loan and the greater likelihood of its repayment being missed. Investors that choose safety above profit may prefer lower-yielding, lower-risk loans.

In conclusion, peer-to-peer (P2P) lending is a novel and potentially lucrative source of passive income that enables investors to lend money directly to borrowers using online platforms. Investors should be aware of the dangers associated with P2P lending even though the returns are larger than those of more conventional types of passive income. Before putting money into peer-to-peer lending, investors should do their homework and determine how much risk they are willing to take.

Methods for Deciding on a Reliable Online Lending Service

P2P lending, often known as marketplace lending, is a newer kind of investing that has gained popularity over the past decade. It's a way to make money by lending money to individuals or small businesses via the internet in exchange for interest payments. For optimal returns, platform selection is as important as it is with any other type of financial commitment.

The performance history of a P2P lending platform should be the primary consideration when making a choice. Successfully connecting borrowers and lenders, as well as paying out investors promptly, are both essential to the platform's credibility. Examining the default rates, late payments, and returns from the platform's past is crucial.

The platform's loans come with a certain amount of risk, so that's something to think about, too. Some platforms offer reduced-risk loans at lower interest rates and others specialize in high-risk loans. Knowing the risk level of each loan and selecting a platform that fits your comfort level with risk is crucial.

Consider the platform's pricing structure as well. Some platforms do not charge costs for loans, some that charge fees for everything from origination to servicing to late payments, and those that charge fees for nothing. When calculating your return on investment, it is crucial to include these expenses.

While choosing a peer-to-peer lending platform, it is also important to consider the quality of the underwriting process. To make sure that only responsible borrowers are given loans, a thorough underwriting process is necessary. A borrower's income, debt, and credit history should all be scrutinized during this procedure.

The quality of the platform's assistance to its users is also crucial. In the event of any problems, a reputable platform will offer speedy and helpful customer support.

Last but not least, you should think about how liquid the loans on the platform are. Secondary markets are a feature of several peer-to-peer lending platforms, where investors can trade in and out of pre-existing loans. This function allows investors more leeway in making decisions about their investments and liquidity if they need to liquidate their loans.

In conclusion, there are several aspects of a P2P lending platform to take into account when making a final decision, such as the platform's reputation, risk, fees and costs, underwriting procedure, customer service, and liquidity. You can find success in P2P lending if you consider all of these variables and then choose a platform that fits in with your investment objectives and comfort level.

Criteria for Judging Loans and Borrowers

P2P (peer-to-peer) lending is the practice of lending money directly to a borrower rather than to a bank or other financial institution. When compared to more conventional investment vehicles, the returns on P2P loans may be significantly higher. But, there are potential downsides, just like any other type of investment. In this section, we'll talk about how P2P lending platforms evaluate borrowers and loans.

Borrowers' creditworthiness is a major factor in loan approval. When determining a borrower's creditworthiness, P2P lending services often look at their credit scores and financial documents. Loan acceptance rates are higher for borrowers with better credit scores because they pose less of a risk to lenders. As a result, some platforms may necessitate more data from borrowers—like income and employment history—to determine their trustworthiness.

There's also the matter of the loan's intended use to think about. Personal loans, business loans, and real estate loans are just a few of the loan categories that some peer-to-peer lending platforms focus on. The borrower's creditworthiness and loan-repayment capacity can be inferred from the loan's stated purpose. Borrowers seeking funds for debt consolidation may be viewed as a lower risk than those seeking capital for a new business endeavor.

The borrower's past payment record is another consideration. The borrower's payment history, including any missing or late payments on previous loans, may be made available through peer-to-peer lending platforms. A borrower who consistently falls short on their loan payments may be seen as riskier.

After a borrower has been assessed and found to be creditworthy, a loan listing will be posted on the P2P lending platform where investors can choose to finance the loan. When investors have this information, they can decide if they want to finance the loan. The amount, interest rate, and length of a loan are just a few of the elements that investors should think about.

The sum of money the borrower wants to get from the lender is called the loan amount. Investors need to weigh the size of the loan against the borrower's financial stability and repayment history. A higher risk may be associated with a loan if the amount requested is disproportionate to the borrower's income and financial stability.

Simply said, the interest rate is the percentage of the loan's principal that the borrower will be responsible for paying each year. To make an informed decision, investors need to weigh the interest rate against the creditworthiness of the borrower and the loan's overall risk. There may be a correlation between loan risk and interest rate.

The duration of time the borrower has to make loan payments is known as the loan term. The risk involved in the loan and the financial stability of the borrower should both be taken into account by investors when determining the loan's tenure. A greater-risk loan could be one with a longer repayment period.

In addition to these considerations, investors need also to think about portfolio diversity. Diversifying your loan portfolio can help mitigate the negative effects of any defaults.

Investors using peer-to-peer lending platforms may be subject to charges including origination fees and servicing costs. It's important to include these costs when calculating a loan's potential ROI.

The investment's liquidity is another important factor for investors to think about. P2P loans are not traded on a public market like stocks and bonds, which can make it more difficult to liquidate the investment in the event of a financial emergency. On some peer-to-peer lending platforms, investors can sell their loans to other investors on a secondary market, albeit this feature is not always available or may come with costs.

Creditworthiness, loan purpose, repayment history, loan size, interest rate, loan length, fees, diversification, and liquidity are just a few of the elements that must be considered when evaluating borrowers and loans on P2P lending platforms. Although peer-to-peer (P2P) lending has the potential for larger returns than more conventional investment vehicles, potential investors should be aware of the dangers involved and conduct extensive research on the companies offering the loans before making any commitments.

Taking Charge of Your Loan Portfolio

P2P lending, often known as "social lending" or "crowdlending," eliminates the need for traditional financial institutions like banks by connecting lenders and borrowers directly. Peer-to-peer lending has been increasingly popular in recent years due to the opportunity it presents for producing passive income. Investors should be aware of the dangers associated with P2P lending.

Selecting a reliable P2P lending platform is an important first step for investors. Many peer-to-peer lending systems exist, each with its own regulations and pricing structures. LendingClub, Prosper, and Upstart are just a few examples of these sites that have found success. You should do your homework on the platforms to locate the one that best fits your investment aims and comfort level with risk before putting any money into it.

After settling on a lending platform, the following step is to investigate the creditworthiness of the borrowers and the loans they have taken out. Typical borrower financial data provided by loan marketplaces include credit score, debt-to-income ratio, work status, and more. Investors can gauge whether or not they think the borrower will be able to pay back the loan based on the data provided.

The period of the loan, the interest rate, and its intended use are all factors that investors should think about. The length of a loan's term, from a few months to several years, and the interest rate charged on that loan, from a low to a high, are both variables that depend on the borrower's creditworthiness. Investors should also consider the loan's intended use, since particular borrowers and lending purposes may provide greater risk. Borrowing money to pay off existing debt may be safer than using the funds to launch a brand-new enterprise.

P2P lending also requires careful management of your loan portfolio. When it comes to peer-to-peer lending, diversification is essential for keeping risks at bay. Diversifying your investments over several loans and debtors will help cushion the blow of any defaults. Lending platforms offer automated solutions that help investors spread their money across multiple assets.

Another approach to increase your profits from P2P lending is to reinvest your money. Returns can typically be immediately reinvested into more loans through most lending systems. You may increase your earnings by reinvesting your money and letting it grow via the power of compounding.

Keeping tabs on your investments is another crucial part of managing your loan portfolio. Investors need to keep tabs on their holdings and be ready to make changes to their portfolios if necessary. Investors should make use of the lending platforms' available tools and reports to monitor their portfolio's success.

Investors should be aware of the dangers associated with P2P lending before considering it as a passive income source. P2P lending portfolio management entails several stages, including picking the correct platform, assessing the borrowers and loans, spreading your money around, reinvesting your profits, and keeping a close eye on your holdings. P2P lending can be a great way to diversify your passive income sources, provided you do your homework and handle the risks involved.

Profitability while limiting exposure to lose.

Social lending, another name for P2P lending, has exploded in popularity as a means for investors to reap the benefits of P2P lending while doing relatively little work. The concept of peer-to-peer (P2P) lending refers to the practice of lending money directly to borrowers over the internet as opposed to through traditional financial institutions like banks.

Here we'll go over several tactics for getting the most out of your P2P lending investments while reducing your risk exposure.

Invest in a variety of different things because, as with any financial decision, diversity pays well. You can spread out your risk by lending small amounts to numerous borrowers. You can lessen your risk associated with any one borrower or platform if you diversify your assets among several loans, borrowers, and platforms.

Choose a trusted platform: While looking for a P2P lending platform, it's crucial to make an informed decision. Choose a service that has been around for a while and can prove its worth. Verify the platform's reputation by reading reviews on third-party sites and looking at its star rating.

Loan kinds come with varying degrees of risk and reward, so it's important to pick wisely. Unsecured loans, for instance, are riskier than secured loans but also typically have higher interest rates. Try to choose loans that have a low default rate and a history of being repaid on time.

Credit scores are assigned to each borrower on P2P platforms to evaluate their risk. Borrowers with a low debt-to-income ratio and a high credit score should be prioritized. You can assess their potential to repay the loan by looking at things like their employment record, income, and so on.

Think about the **underwriting requirements of the platform** you're interested in. Choose a service that does extensive checks on the loans it produces and has a robust process for vetting borrowers.

Returns on this investment, like those on other forms of investments, can be increased through reinvestment. You may compound your gains and grow your portfolio with the help of most P2P platforms' automatic reinvestment features.

Even though P2P lending can provide a steady stream of passive income, it is still vital to keep tabs on your assets from time to time. Always keep an eye on your loan portfolio to make sure everything is running well. An increased rate of defaults, for example, might signal a potential need to reevaluate your investment approach.

Although P2P lending is a great way to generate passive income, it's crucial to **keep your expectations in check.** You shouldn't count on getting rich quickly, and you should also be ready for some of your loans to go into default. There is always going to be a degree of risk involved with every investment you make.

For those interested in passive income, P2P lending can be a terrific option, but it's crucial to go into it with a well-thought-out investment plan and reasonable expectations. Investment returns and losses can be optimized through careful portfolio diversification, careful selection of loan kinds, careful assessment of borrower risk, and vigilant monitoring of all investments.

CHAPTER 9

Optimizing Your Sources of Passive Income

1. Multiplying Your Sources of Passive Income
2. Generating Passive Income Via Automation
3. Financial Planning for Passive Income
4. Using Passive Income to Fund Retirement
5. Using Passive Income to Create Generational Wealth

Multiplying Your Sources of Passive Income

It's possible to make money with little to no work by generating passive income. Many strive to develop many, stable sources of passive income because of the security and freedom it can give. But after you have a few passive income streams developed, scaling them up to optimize earnings is the next stage. The following are some suggestions for expanding your sources of passive income:

Grow your current revenue sources.

Growing your current passive income sources is the quickest and most straightforward approach to scaling your business. Methods that can help achieve this goal include producing additional content, ramping up promotional activities, and expanding the range of goods and services on offer. To increase your passive income from affiliate marketing, for instance, you may promote more products, make more content, and attract more visitors.

Make some new channels

Adding additional streams is another strategy for growing your passive income. This can be accomplished through the investigation of untapped markets, the formation of strategic alliances with other artists and businesses, and the introduction of brand-new products and services. You can increase your passive income from, say, rental homes, by buying more of them or branching out into commercial real estate.

Subcontract and mechanize

Assisting you in growing your passive revenue streams, outsourcing and automation are potent instruments. Both outsourcing and automation involve relying on third parties to carry out previously performed duties. With the time and effort, you save using either of these strategies, you'll be able to devote more of your resources to other endeavors, such as expanding your passive income streams.

Improve your abilities by spending time and money on them.

Improving your knowledge and abilities can also help you increase your passive income. If you're making money on the side as a software developer, for instance, you may use that money into expanding your knowledge of programming languages, tools, and frameworks so you can make even more money.

Create a group

Last but not least, assembling a group is a great way to increase the size of your passive income. You can get help with marketing, content development, customer service, and accountancy, among other things, by hiring employees or independent contractors. This will allow you to devote more resources to strategic endeavors, like expanding your firm.

Increasing your passive income streams will need time, effort, and commitment on your part. You can reach your financial goals and benefit from a diversified and sustainable passive income portfolio if you adopt the right mindset and approach to investing.

Generating Passive Income Via Automation

People in today's fast-paced society are constantly on the lookout for easy methods to monetize their time. One common strategy for accomplishing this is to rely on passive income sources, which provide financial support without requiring the recipient to perform any labor on their part. Real estate, stocks and bonds, intellectual property, affiliate marketing, and peer-to-peer lending are just some of the many potential sources of passive income.

You can scale up your efforts once you've established a passive revenue source or several. Building long-term wealth and achieving financial independence requires scaling your passive income streams. Increasing revenue can be accomplished by developing both existing and new revenue sources.

Increasing your investment capital is one strategy for growing your passive income streams. You can buy more rental properties and expand your rental portfolio if you invest in real estate, for instance. If your online course does well, you can expand your business by making other such courses.

Increasing your marketing efforts is another great approach to growing your passive income sources. To earn more money as an affiliate marketer, you need to broaden your audience, produce higher-quality content, and promote your affiliate items more actively. It is possible to expand your customer base through the use of digital marketing strategies like social media, email, and so on.

A second factor in successfully expanding your operations is automating your passive income streams. Automating your revenue streams is a great way to save time and effort while ensuring a steady supply of cash. Software automation makes it possible to do things like manage rental properties, monitor stock and bond holdings, and coordinate affiliate marketing initiatives.

Also, you may streamline your P2P lending activities by making use of automated investment platforms that do the legwork of finding and funding the finest loans for you. By freeing up your time and energy to focus on other vital chores and investments, automating your passive income streams can help you attain financial freedom.

When trying to increase your passive income, it's crucial to remember that diversification is key. There is a direct correlation between the number of passive income sources in your portfolio and the amount of risk and return you experience. To diversify your portfolio, you might, for instance, put money into both real estate and equities and bonds.

Last but not least, it is critical to monitor your passive income sources and assess their efficacy regularly. If you want to maximize your profits and cut your losses, you need to examine your income streams, expenses, and returns. If you take the time to assess your passive income streams regularly, you can pinpoint opportunities for growth and take corrective action to maximize your passive income.

Scaling your passive income streams is crucial to building lasting wealth and reaching your financial independence goals. You may reach your financial goals, sleep better at night, and have more peace of mind by investing more, optimizing your marketing, automating your efforts, diversifying your portfolio, and assessing your results.

Financial Planning for Passive Income

Passive income is a fantastic way to make money with little to no effort. To be sure, though, you know how your passive income will be taxed, it's crucial. You may have to pay taxes on your passive income if it meets certain criteria.

Here we'll talk about ways to minimize your tax liability from passive income.

The Tax System and Tax Brackets

Knowing your tax bracket is essential to estimate your tax liability from passive income. A tax bracket is the level of income between which a different tax rate begins to apply. Income tax rates in the United States are progressive, meaning that they increase as one's salary rises.

If you are a single taxpayer with $100,000 in passive income, for instance, you will pay 24% tax on your earnings. Your tax liability on passive income will thus be 24%.

Incurred Costs That May Be Deducted

The ability to deduct certain costs from your taxable income is a major perk of earning passive income. Some examples of this kind of expenditure are the price of maintaining a rental property, the price of managing a stock portfolio, or the price of creating materials for an online course.

Keep in mind that there are rules set forth by the IRS regarding deductions. When filing a deduction, make sure you fully grasp the applicable regulations.

Depreciation

Depreciation can be used to lower taxable income for property owners who also rent out their properties. You can deduct the cost of an asset over its useful life through a taxing process known as depreciation.

If you possess a rental property with a $200,000 value, for instance, you can write it off as an expense over 27.5 years. As a result, you can reduce your yearly taxable income by about $7,272.

Individual Retirement Accounts (IRAs)

Putting money into tax-deferred retirement plans, such as an IRA or 401(k), is another way to lower your effective tax rate on passive income. You can avoid paying taxes on the money you put into these accounts until you withdraw it in retirement.

You can potentially cut your tax rate and increase your take-home pay by investing in tax-deferred accounts.

Consumption-based losses in passive income

It's possible to reduce your taxable income by the number of losses you incur from passive sources of income. You can deduct losses from businesses and investments from your taxable income.

To be clear, there are restrictions on how much of your passive income you can deduct. There are limits to how much and how you can deduct losses, as set by the Internal Revenue Service.

Paying Taxes on Capital Gains

Capital gains taxes apply to earnings from the sale of assets like stocks and real estate that are held for more than a year. Gains from the sale of assets are subject to a tax known as capital gains tax.

Capital gains tax rates vary by how long an asset was held. Short-term capital gains are taxed at your regular income tax rate, and they apply if you've held the asset for less than a year. Long-term capital gains taxes, which are levied on asset sales after more than a year of ownership, are generally lower than regular income taxes.

In conclusion, passive income generation is a fantastic method of making money with comparatively little work. To be sure, though, you know how your passive income will be taxed, it's crucial. You may minimize your tax liability and increase your profits by familiarizing yourself with tax brackets, deductible expenses, depreciation, tax-deferred retirement accounts, passive income losses, and capital gains taxes. Make sure you talk to a tax expert to figure out the best tax methods for you.

Using Passive Income to Fund Retirement

To guarantee one's future financial stability, retirement planning is a crucial step. One strategy for doing so is to set up passive income streams that can bring in money long after retirement has begun. This chapter will discuss how passive income can be used in retirement preparation.

Passive income is advantageous because it can supply a reliable flow of funds to support other forms of retirement planning. Traditional retirement savings plans like 401(k)s and IRAs won't be sufficient to pay all of your retirement needs, especially if you have a longer life expectancy than average. A more secure retirement income can be secured by establishing several passive income streams.

Leasing real estate is one way to set up a system of passive income generation. Due to its potential for both capital appreciation and stable rental income, real estate is a common choice among those saving for retirement. If you hire a property manager to handle the day-today maintenance of your rental properties, you can continue to collect rent long after you've officially retired.

Diversify your portfolio with equities and bonds that offer dividends. Companies generally distribute dividends to shareholders regularly, which can provide a reliable source of income. Since bondholders get interest payments regularly, they can be a good option for those seeking a passive income stream.

Another way to make money Passively is through peer-to-peer lending. You can earn money on your investment in P2P loans without having to actively handle the loans yourself. This reduces the dangers of investing in more conventional ways while yet providing a respectable rate of return.

Passive income can also be generated through the development and commercialization of intellectual property. All printed materials, digital materials, and digitally delivered content (such as courses) are included. You can earn money without actively managing the sale process if you develop digital products that can be sold online. Particularly useful for retirees who wish to maintain a steady income stream but who are unable to commit to full-time employment is this option.

The tax ramifications of relying on passive income during retirement are something to think about. The government could tax some forms of passive income at a higher rate than others. For example, the rental income tax rate is often greater than the rate on capital gains from investments like stocks and bonds. If you want to optimize your retirement funds, it's a good idea to talk to a tax expert about how to structure your tax affairs best to take advantage of the passive income streams you'll be generating.

The level of risk attached to any potential source of passive income is another factor to think about. Even though some investments have the potential to yield better profits, they also carry a greater degree of danger. To reduce losses and increase gains, portfolio diversification is crucial.

In conclusion, a more secure financial future can be achieved through retirement planning with passive income. One can augment their retirement savings with a steady stream of income from various passive income sources by diversifying their income streams and managing their investments wisely. If you want to retire comfortably, you should sit down with a financial planner to discuss your options for generating passive income and create a long-term financial strategy that accounts for your various needs and goals.

Using Passive Income to Create Generational Wealth

For oneself and future generations, wealth creation can be greatly aided by passive income. Having a secure financial future, one that you can pass on to your children and grandkids, begins with establishing a steady flow of passive income. In this piece, we'll talk about how to use passive income to leave a legacy of wealth to future generations.

The first step is to identify sources of passive income with the longevity to keep bringing in money for a long time. One excellent example of a passive revenue source that can be relied on for decades, even generations, is a rental property. A well-maintained rental property can provide income for you and your family for decades and can even be included in your will and passed on to your offspring.

Building wealth to pass down through the generations can also be accomplished through prudent investment in stocks, bonds, and other securities. To build a sustainable stream of passive income over the long term, invest in firms with a track record of consistent growth and dividend payments.

Developing intellectual property that may be licensed or sold is another strategy for passing on a fortune to future generations through passive income. This could be anything from penning a book to developing a piece of software that can be sold under a license. The ability to make something of lasting significance can provide financial security for your loved ones for decades.

After determining the best avenues through which to generate passive income, the next stage is to formulate a strategy for transferring your money to future generations. Including your sources of passive income in your will is an easy method to accomplish this. To minimize taxes on the transfer of wealth to future generations, consider establishing a trust or other legal structure.

Another choice is to establish a firm that can be handed down from one generation to the next. It could be a stock portfolio, a real estate investment firm, or even a brand-new corporation. You can leave a lasting legacy for future generations by establishing a company that will provide your family with passive income for many years.

Strategies for creating generational wealth with passive income include estate planning, launching a family company, and buying stocks in companies with high dividend yields. One is passing on financial and investment knowledge to future generations. You may set them up for a lifetime of financial security by instructing them in the ways of passive income and sound fiscal management.

Building a culture of fiscal responsibility among family members is still another option. You can help your kids and grandkids become financially independent and successful in the long run by teaching them to make sound financial decisions from an early age.

As a last thought, keep in mind that generating money that may be passed down through the generations through passive income takes time. Developing a sustainable source of passive income that lasts for decades requires time and perseverance. Nonetheless, it is feasible to leave a legacy of money to your family with the appropriate approaches and a dedication to long-term financial planning.

CHAPTER 10

Last Thoughts

1. Important Takeaways

2. Motivating Ideas and Words of Advice for Getting Things Done

3. Methods and Materials for Generating Passive Income

Important Takeaways

In the final chapter of the guide to passive income, the most important ideas are summarized. This chapter emphasizes passive income's role in securing one's financial independence and provides a brief review of the various passive income streams covered elsewhere in the manual.

One of the most important lessons to be learned from the guide is the significance of determining one's risk tolerance and establishing long-term passive income goals before making any investments in passive income streams. If you want to maximize your return on investment, you need to select passive income streams that are a good fit for your needs and investment preferences.

Although investing in real estate can provide a stable passive income, it's important to pick the right kind of property. While investing in real estate, it is equally important to think about financing and choosing the correct property.

Stocks and bonds are another common way to generate passive income, but it's important to spread your investments around to reduce your exposure to market fluctuations. Investment returns can be increased by the creation of a diverse portfolio, the efficient management of that portfolio, and the reinvestment of dividends.

Passive income can also be generated through the sale of intellectual property such as books, online courses, and software licenses. To optimize earnings, however, you must have a firm grasp of the intellectual property landscape and the prerequisites for licensing.

Some common forms of passive revenue generation include affiliate marketing and P2P lending. Key elements in maximizing returns and avoiding risk include picking the correct programs and platforms, making excellent content to sell products, analyzing borrowers and loans, and monitoring the loan portfolio.

If you want to achieve financial independence, you must learn to scale and automate your passive income streams. Important factors to think about include tax planning, saving for retirement, and passing on wealth through passive income streams.

The necessity of having a plan, defining goals, evaluating risk, and making the appropriate investing decisions are all stressed throughout the course. To maximize profits and avoid risks, it stresses the importance of maintaining a diversified portfolio, exercising proper portfolio management, and keeping abreast of the most recent market trends and conditions.

Motivating Ideas and Words of Advice for Getting Things Done

Congratulations on reading "The Power of Passive Income" You should start constructing your portfolio now that you have a firm grasp of the many potential passive income streams at your disposal.

Always keep in mind that the key to achieving your goals with passive income is, to begin with, a modest investment and expanding it over time. Don't expect quick success; it takes time, effort, and patience to create a steady stream of passive income.

Motivating yourself and keeping your sights on the prize are two of the most crucial steps you can take. Remind yourself of the long-term benefits you and your loved ones will reap from your efforts to create passive income. Make your objectives distinct and build a strategy to reach them.

Maintaining a steady work ethic is crucial to reaching your goals. Schedule some time every day or week to focus on developing passive income sources. Be consistent and make it a habit.

Don't close yourself off from possibilities and don't stop trying to improve. Be bold and explore different avenues. Don't be afraid to change your strategy if it's not working.

Last but not least, remember to reward yourself for your efforts along the way. It's vital to stop and celebrate the small wins along the way as you work to build your passive income stream.

Build a passive income portfolio that will offer you and your family financial security and independence for years to come through hard work, tenacity, and a willingness to learn and adapt. Exactly how long are you going to wait? Today is the day to get moving!

Methods and Materials for Generating Passive Income

Here, you'll find a comprehensive list of useful websites, apps, and other assets that can be used in the process of creating and maintaining passive income streams. Websites, apps, and printed books all exist that provide helpful guidance and materials for anyone seeking to establish passive income streams.

This chapter highlights internet markets like Amazon and eBay as some valuable resources. Books, e-books, audiobooks, and other forms of digital media can all be sold on these websites since they provide a venue for independent vendors to do so. Fulfillment by Amazon (FBA) and eBay Valet are two of the services provided by Amazon and eBay that facilitate the creation and management of an online store.

Usefulness of financial management software as a resource for individuals are also highlighted. Popular solutions like Mint, Personal Capital, and Quicken are among these tools because of their ability to assist people to manage their money and keep track of their spending and savings. Those who are responsible for many passive income streams and who need to be organized and informed about their money may find these tools very helpful.

Several publications and websites that contain helpful information and resources for establishing passive income streams, in addition to online marketplaces and software packages are recommended here. Sites like Investopedia, BiggerPockets, and Smart Passive Income are frequently cited as helpful resources for learning about and establishing passive income strategies. Books like "The 4-Hour Work Week" by Tim Ferriss and "The Passive Income Playbook" by Raza Imam are suggested because they provide actionable advice and proven methods for creating passive income streams with minimal effort.

This chapter also emphasizes the value of establishing connections with other people who share your interests and goals. Participating in events, networks, and communities that can help you earn passive income and launch your own business are all good places to start. Mutually beneficial partnerships can be invaluable resources for anyone attempting to create and oversee many passive income streams.

Finally, readers are advised to use analytics and split testing software to monitor and improve their passive income. With these instruments, one can assess the efficacy of one's marketing efforts and make educated choices concerning the enhancement of one's passive revenue streams.

In conclusion, the tools and resources discussed here provide a wealth of information and support for anyone seeking to construct and maintain their passive income streams. These tools, which range from online markets and financial management software to networking and relationship-building, can aid individuals in establishing secure and independent passive income streams over time.

CONCLUSIONS AND FUTURE DIRECTIONS

Congratulations! Congratulations, you have concluded this wonderful guide. You now know how to get started with several distinct passive income streams.

You should now have a firm grasp of why it's crucial to establish many streams of passive income and how doing so can set you on the path to financial independence. You may have also determined the sources of passive income that are consistent with your way of life, risk preferences, and financial objectives.

To be sure, this is only the start. Learning, experimenting, and hard effort is necessary when constructing passive revenue streams. No promises of easy money or rapid success can be made. Yet if you put in the time, effort, and persistence, passive income can be yours.

So, tell me, what are you going to do now? Some ideas are as follows:

If you want to succeed at earning passive income, you need to make sure your goals are SMART (specific, measurable, attainable, relevant, and timely). Put them on paper and divide the process into manageable chunks. This will assist in maintaining your concentration and drive.

The only way to create passive revenue streams is to actively pursue them. You should get started by focusing on one or two passive income streams that speak to you. Just do it; don't sit around waiting for the right moment. Use what you have to get going, and then upgrade as you go.

You shouldn't have to re-create the wheel if you can learn from others' experiences. Examine the strategies of those who have already achieved success in creating passive income sources. Spend time with like-minded people through learning from books, podcasts, seminars, and online forums.

Maintain a log of your accomplishments so that you may look back on your progress, make any necessary strategy changes, and revel in your successes. You'll be able to keep your drivers up and make wiser choices as a result.

Don't give up; it will take time and effort to set up passive revenue streams. Make sure you don't give up too soon. Continue working toward your objectives, expanding your knowledge, and taking positive action.

You can also check out some resources and tools to assist you to create passive income streams, in addition to these measures.

Here are a few sources you can consult:

Courses may be found all over the internet, and many of them focus on the topic of creating passive income. Everything from real estate investing to affiliate marketing is covered in these classes, both as individual topics and as broad categories. Pick a program that works for your schedule and budget.

Financial instruments: a wide variety of financial instruments exist to aid in the management of passive income streams. Apps to keep tabs on spending and investments and tax calculators are all examples of such aids.

The use of an online marketplace, such as Amazon, Etsy, or Fiverr, can help you reach a larger customer base and promote your business to a greater number of people. These sites give you instant access to a large target audience and a streamlined system for making sales.

Services to outsource: As your passive income sources expand, you may find that you need to hire help to keep up with everything. Content production, client support, and advertising are just some of the many functions that can be outsourced.

In nut shell, if you want to be financially independent, then you should work toward that goal by creating multiple streams of passive income. Keep in mind that there is no cookie-cutter method for establishing many streams of passive income. Pick the methods that work best for you and your interests and abilities and keep pushing forward. You can achieve long-term financial independence and security by accumulating several passive income streams, given the proper attitude, resources, and tools.